CW00433676

The Up-
Pekingese

By
Lillian C. Raymond Mallock

Vintage Dog Books
Home Farm
44 Evesham Road
Cookhill, Alcester
Warwickshire
B49 5LJ

www.vintagedogbooks.com

ISBN No. 978-1-84664-066-7(Paperback)
978-1-84664-067-4 (Hardback)

Published by Vintage Dog Books 2006
Vintage Dog books is an imprint of Read Books

British Library Cataloguing-in-Publication Data
A catalogue record for this book is available
from the British Library.

Vintage Dog Books
Home Farm
44 Evesham Road
Cookhill, Alcester
Warwickshire
B49 5LJ

THOMAS FALL,

Photographer,

9, BAKER ST., LONDON, W.

MANY of the Illustrations in these pages are from Photos by Mr. FALL, who has had a very wide experience, and is specially equipped for Photographing Pekingese.

The Photos are taken either in Studio or at the Kennels by arrangement.

Mrs. RAYMOND-MALLOCK WITH THREE OF HER WINNING PEKINGESE.

THE
Up-to-Date Pekingese
AND
All other Toy Dogs.

The History, Points, and Standards of Pekingese, Toy Spaniels, Japanese, Pomeranians, Yorkshire and Toy Terriers, Schipperkes, Pugs, Griffon Bruxellois, Maltese and Italian Greyhounds, with instructive chapters on Breeding, Rearing, Feeding, Training and Showing ; and full information as to treatment of most ailments.

WRITTEN AND PUBLISHED
BY
LILLIAN C. RAYMOND-MALLOCK,

2, PRESTON PARK AVENUE,
BRIGHTON, ENGLAND.

Phone, Preston 3561.

REVISED EDITION.   ILLUSTRATED.

Price   -   -   -   -   -   7/6
United States   -   -   -   *Two Dollars*

PREFACE.

IN giving my experiences to the public, I do so with a view to preventing the novice from tumbling into the many pitfalls which beset my path. Although I had been accustomed to dogs from early childhood, when their management had to come under my personal supervision I felt the need, which I am now trying to supply to others, of some practical hints and simple remedies for the many common ailments of my small charges. All of the remedies given have been used successfully in my kennel, and several are original, and are now made public for the first time.

NOTE TO THIRD EDITION.

In bringing out this further edition of "Toy Dogs," I must thank the many readers who have taken the trouble to write and let me know that they had found the book useful, and have thereby encouraged me to continue its existence and to bring it more up-to-date. Chapters have been added which have been the result of further experience, and the advent of new remedies.

LILLIAN C. RAYMOND-MALLOCK.

DEDICATED TO

MRS. ARMAR CORRY.

TABLE OF CONTENTS.

The Various Breeds.

General Care.

Diseases and Treatment.

THE DIRECTORY OF BREEDERS.

Pekingese.

Mr. Mose Bloom, 1, Castle Street, Pentreback, Merthyr Tydfil.
Miss Brunker, Whippendell House, King's Langley.
Mrs. Bines, 176, St. Helen's Street, Ipswich.
Mrs. Birch, 67, Tixall Road, Stafford.
Mrs. L. Bibby, 1, Water Street, Charleston, West. Va., U.S.A.
Miss Boyes-Smith, 74A, Malden Road, Brighton.
Mrs. Clapham, Luneville, near Warberry, Torquay.
Mrs. Shelly-Creek, Agardsly, Sutton, Coldfield.
Mrs. Cecil, 21, Ennismore Gardens, London, S.W.
Miss Currie, Bonheur, Beckley, East Surrey.
Mrs. Colleson, 56, Leopold Street, Leeds.
Mrs. Cockburn, Whitworth House, Bedlington.
Mrs. Cross-Barratt, Bon Air, St. Saviours, Jersey, C.I.
Miss Carter, Salmonky Rectory, Horncastle.
Miss Dutfield, 168, Alexandra Road, Heely, Sheffield.
Mrs. Dalglish, 16, Mansions House Drive, Shettleston, Glasgow.
Miss Dingley, 1151, Washington Street, So. Braintree, Mass., U.S.A.
Mr. G. H. Eddleston, 28, Manley Road, Oldham.
Mr. C. Farney-Brown, 4, Colborne Road, Brighton.
Miss Fraser, Landsdowne, Haywards Heath.
Mrs. Fothergill, Castle Cottage, Aynam Road, Kendal.
Mrs. B. Foster, c/o Mrs. Walker, 781, Gerrard St., E. Toronto,
    Phone, 5099 W.
Mrs. Grimwood, 104, Ashburton Avenue, Croydon, Surrey.
Mr. A. E. Gazzard, 760, Chesterfield Road.,Woodseats, Sheffield.
Mrs. R. A. Gibbons, 29, Cadogan Place, S.W.
Miss Goodwin, Tripleton, Henwick, near Worcester.
Mrs. H. R. Gordon, 14, Abbotsbury Road, Weymouth.
Mrs. A. H. Gent, Warrenhurst, Barton-on-Sea, New Milton.
Mr. Greenall, 36, Havelock Square, Sheffield.
Mrs. Jardine Gresson, Stoke House, Severn, Stoke, Worcestershire.
Mrs. Harris, 12, Spencer Gardens, Eltham.
Miss Hillman, 15, Tennis Road, Hove.
Miss Hancock, 77, Albany Mansions, Albert Bridge Rd., London, S.W.
Mrs. Haslock, Kenley House, Kenley, Surrey.
Miss Hevston, St. David's, Greystones, Co. Wicklow.
Mrs. H. Hutley, Well House, 57, Meadow Road, Leeds.
Mrs. Jenny, Kenilworth House, Thetford, Horncastle.
Mrs. Jacklin, Craven House, Belle Vue, Wakefield.
Miss Duffield Jones, Melville Lodge, Bognor.
Mrs. Jarvis, 2624E, 26, St. Sheepshead Bay, New York.
Mrs. Key, Sundridge, near Sevenoaks.
Mrs. Kinden-Carter, 20, Downshire Hill, Hampstead, N.W.
Mrs. Lambert, 3, Lyall Ave., Longue Point, Montreal, Canada.
Mrs. Lister, Bag-Enderby Rectory, Spilsky.
Mrs. Luff, Red Lion Inn, St. Pancras, Chichester.
Mr. Le Bert, Newlands, Woodland Rd., Colwyn Bay.

Mrs. Miles, The Aviaries, Chichester.
Miss L. Morgan, 108, Craiglea Street, Edinburgh.
Mrs. Maughan, Tetford House, Horncastle.
Mrs. P. Morrell, Burton Vicarage Neston, Chester.
Mrs. Marie May, 72, Huron Road. Tooting Common, London.
Mrs. Nadin, Brierley Hall, near Barnsley.
Mrs. Montgomery Neilson, 20, Richmond Road, Exeter.
Mrs. Perelli, 51, Cleveland Road, Brighton.
Mrs. Pomfrett, 10, Barry Street, Warrington.
Miss Patrick, Bally Duff, S.O. Co. Waterford.
Mrs. Wm. Perry, 123, Grove Avenue, Leominster, Mass. U.S.A.
Miss Polak, Brattleborough, Surrenden Rd., Brighton.
Miss Rawson, 77, Granville Street, Boston, Lincoln.
Mrs. Richards, 15 Sutherland Place, Bayswater.
Mrs. Jack Sarjeant, Rustington, Westcliff, Eastbourne.
Mrs. Shrubb, 94, Pretoria Road, Streatham Park, S.W.16.
Miss Spink-Shaw, 9, Rugby Place, Kemp Town, Brighton.
Madame Scheibe, 28, Elliot Road, Thornton Heath, Surrey.
Mrs. Shepherd, Pekin, Clarendon Road, Luton.
Miss Treasure, 15, Margaret Street, Bayonne, N.J., U.S.A.
Miss Thomas, Riverview, Castletownroche, Cork.
Mrs. Turner-Hackwood, Riversleigh, Beckenham, Kent.
Mrs. Tate, St. Quentin, Nami Tal, India.
Mrs. Harold Taylor, Prospect House, Lostock, near Bolton.
Miss Tubbs, 137, Walm Lane, Cricklewood, N.W.2.
Mrs. Wilson, 13A, Rawson Street, Halifax.
Mrs. Worrall, 29, Trinity Square, Brixton, S.W.1.
Mrs. Wood-Webster, 27, Birch Grove, Benton, Newcastle.
Mrs. Wallace, Monkwearmouth and Southwick, Sunderland.
Mrs. Woo, 606, 10th Avenue, So., Minneapolis, Minn., U.S.A.
Mrs. Woodfin, Fairholme, Bexley, Kent.
Yorkdale Kennels, 3540, Wilton Avenue, Chicago, U.S.A.

Toy Spaniels.

Mrs. Clements, 6, Kirby Road, Leicester.
Mrs. Herbert Haigh, Cold Ithel, Llandogo, near Chepstowe.
Mr. J. Kennedy, 8, Cottage Gardens, Murrayfield, Edinburgh.
Mr. Lewis, Marlborough Kennels, Gray Creek, B.C., Canada.
Mrs. Maughan, Tetford House, Horncastle.
Mrs. Rollo-Stewart, 17, Kingsburgh Road, Murrayfield, Edinburgh.

Japanese.

Mrs. Cooper, 8, Beech Grove, Beverley Road, Hull.
Mrs. A. H. Gent, Warrenhurst, Barton-on-Sea, New Milton.

Pomeranians.

Mrs. Judge Brown, 55, Ladywell Road, S.E.13.
Mr. J. Messenger, 90, Stanforth Rd., Birmingham.
Miss C. Smith, 36, Monkton Street, Ryde, I. of Wight.

Miss Woods, Greenmount, Clonsella, Co. Dublin.
Miss L. Wilson, Shaws Corner House, Redhill, Surrey.
Mrs. Cockburn, 9, Brunswick Square, W.C.1.

Griffons.

Mrs. Bate, Church House, Chudleigh Knighton, near Newton Abbot.
Miss Croucher, 6, Burlington Place, Eastbourne.
Mrs. Rollo-Stewart, 17, Kingsburgh Road, Murrayfield, Edinburgh.
Mrs. C. Morgan, Restharrow, Charterhouse Hill, Godalming, Surrey.
Miss Patrick, Bally Duff, S.O., Co. Waterford.

Yorkshire.

Mrs. Maughan, Tetford House, Horncastle.

Toy Dogs.

Mr. J. W. Gardiner, P.O. box 4, Dallas, Texas, U.S.A.

Notice.

The picture of Ashton-More Chu Chi on the cover of this book, together with many other of the illustrations are from photos by Mr. Fall of 9, Baker Street, London, W.

x.

THE PEKINGESE.

The Legend of the Origin of Pekingese.

In China there is a Patron Saint of Animals, by name Ah Chu. One day a King among Lions went to consult Ah Chu upon a very important matter—" Might he marry a Marmoset ? " to which Ah Chu replied " Yes, upon the condition that you will sacrifice your strength and your size for the sake of Love." The noble Lion accepted the sacrifice, and gave his heart into the keeping of the tiny Marmoset. The result of their marriage was the Pekingese. To this day we can trace in them the tenderness and beauty of the Marmoset eye, and the gorgeous ruff and noble dignity of the Monarch among Beasts.

Ch. Goodwood Lo.

The History of the Breed.

The breed is of great antiquity ; in fact, it is impossible to go back far enough to discover its origin ; but we know that this Royal breed of dog has existed from time immemorial in the Imperial palaces of the Celestial Empire, and at the looting of the Summer Palace at Pekin by the " foreign devils " bronze effigies of these dogs were discovered known to be 2,000 years old. They have also been found represented in all kinds of antique Chinese art, and may be seen carved in stone at the entrance of many an old temple, or exquisitely portrayed in rare porcelains and tapestries. In all these there is no mistaking the idol of the Imperial drawingroom, with his short bowed legs, sturdy lion-like figure, swaying plume, profuse mane, large prominent eyes, and broad forehead. These little creatures have always been most jealously guarded, and few have ever found their way into the outer world ; they were kept under the care of special attendants, who were answerable for their safety with their lives. The penalty for the theft of one of them was a series of frightful tortures, culminating in death. It was therefore impossible to obtain a specimen of the true Palace dog for love or money, but at the looting of the Summer Palace at Pekin, during the occupation of the city by the Allies in 1860, five of these carefully-guarded mites were forgotten in the hurried flight of the Court. They were discovered in a portion of the garden said to be the favourite retreat of the Emperor's Aunt, who committed suicide on the approach of the troops. Admiral Lord John Hay and another Naval Officer (a relative of the late Duke of Richmond), who were present at the time, each secured two, those of the latter founding the famous Goodwood strain. The fifth specimen was obtained by Gen. Dunn, who, on his arrival in England, presented the little creature to her Majesty Queen Victoria. It was a beautiful fawn and white, and was very small and attractive. Its portrait was subsequently painted for the Queen by Landseer, and is now said to be at Windsor Castle. The colour of the other dogs was a golden sable or rich chestnut brown, with black markings, and they weighed from 4 to 6 lbs. each. As far as we can ascertain, these five were the only Pekin Palace or Sacred Temple Dogs which reached England for many years, and to them a large proportion of the modern dogs trace their descent. Several unsuccessful attempts were made to secure other specimens from the Palace, but it was not until 1896 that Mrs. Douglas Murray finally succeeded in importing a pair direct from the Imperial Precincts, supposed to have been smuggled away with great difficulty and no little ingenuity. These were the well known Ah Cum and Mimosa, which weighed on their arrival in England 5 and 3 lbs. respectively. The dog was bred to several of the Goodwood strain, and in the first litters Ch. Goodwood Lo and Goodwood Put Sing were produced. These two and their father all become famous sires, and most of the purest strains of to-day include them among their progenitors. Ah Cum lived until a few years ago. He was a true sleeve dog, and almost perfect in all points. His effigy can be seen stuffed in the South Kensington Museum. In Pekin the very small specimens are called sleeve dogs, as they were carried about by the Court ladies in the ample sleeves of their wonderful Chinese costumes. To breed a perfect sleeve dog is the height of ambition to most fanciers, but alas, it is not easy to do, and it seems well nigh impossible to produce a Pekingese weighing under 5 lbs. which is good in all-round points. Some very tiny ones have been exhibited, but they are usually weedy and untypical. The most useful size appears to be from 7 to 9 lbs., and there are plenty of good dogs between these weights. In Pekin the diminutive specimens are most greatly prized, and the smaller they are the better. We have heard almost incredible stories as to the extreme minuteness of some of the Empress's prime favourites. It may be well to mention here before proceeding further with the history of these quaint little fellows, that they must not be confused with the Pekin Spaniel, a coarser and much larger dog, which though having many similar characteristics, is a distinct breed. They are quite common in many Chinese towns, and can be imported without difficulty. The following is an extract from a letter which bears on this point, written by Lord John Hay and published in " The New Book of the Dog " :—" Now there is another breed which is confounded with the Palace Dog. They present the same characteristics, and appear very similar, disposition equally charming, but they are much larger ; they are also called Pekin Spaniels ; but they are as different breeds originally, I feel sure, as a Pegu pony is from an English hunter. They are seldom so well provided with hair on the feet, and the ' trousers ' do not go down far enough ; also the hair on stomach and sides does not grow long enough." It will be seen from the above authority that the fact of a dog having been imported from Pekin, is no criterion that it is one of the much-prized Palace pets ; and I think it is well to emphasise this fact here, and to dispel the existing impressions which are general with reference to the majority of imported dogs.

As far as we know the early history of the breed in England dates from the foundation of the Goodwood Kennel, and from Mrs. Douglas Murray's and Mrs. Allen's imported dogs. The latter lady was, I believe, the first to exhibit " Pekes " in England, and her Pekin Paul, who was shown at Chester in 1894, was looked upon as a great curiosity. From this small beginning the breed increased rapidly, and in 1898 the standard of points was drawn up, and revised two years later. The interests of the breed was then looked after by the Japanese Spaniel Club, but in 1902 The Pekingese Club was inaugurated, and later in 1908

The Ashton-More Pekingese.

ASHTON-MORE HEIN-SU.

ASHTON-MORE WEN-CHU.

Owned and Bred by Mrs. Raymond Mallock, 2, Preston Park Avenue, Brighton.

The Ashton-More Pekingese.

KWAI-KWAI OF EGHAM.

ASHTON-MORE FOO-KWAI.

Owned and Bred by Mrs. Raymond Mallock, 2, Preston Park Avenue, Brighton.

The Ashton-More Pekingese.

ASHTON-MORE WEN-TI.
By Nanking Wen Chu and Ashton-More Kinwha.

ASHTON-MORE WEN-FUH.
By Ch. Nanking Wen-ti and Ashton-More Hara.

Owned and Bred by Mrs. Raymond Mallock, 2, Preston Park Avenue, Brighton.

The Ashton-More Pekingese.

ASHTON-MORE CHU-CHI,

ASHTON-MORE CHU-CHI.
Owned by Mrs. Raymond Mallock, 2, Preston Park Avenue Brighton.

The Pekin Palace Dog Association was founded by Lady Algernon Gordon Lennox. From the very first these quaint little dogs were great favourites, and on looking back over the past 15 years, the way in which the breed has increased and multiplied seems almost incredible. Pekingese are to-day quite the most popular Toy variety in England, and larger prices have been obtained for them, taken all round, than for any breed in existence. They are always one of the best supported sections at the great English shows, and although no longer a novelty, always attract a great deal of attention and admiration. The classification is usually a liberal one, consisting of special classes for the different varieties of colour, and often weight classes as well. The subject of weight seems a matter of considerable discussion. Originally the Pekingese Club fixed the maximum weight at 10 lbs., and this was then considered quite heavy enough ; later on, however, the maximum weight was increased to 18 lbs., which, of course, let in a great number of the larger and coarser stamp of dog. The original Palace dog was a diminutive animal, and had bred true to type for many centuries, but with the importation of the larger Pekin Spaniel came the demand for the increased weight. This concession was thought by many fanciers to be very much to the detriment of the breed, and it was on this account that the Pekin Palace Dog Association was formed. The object of this Club is to encourage the original type, and in their standard of points they have fixed the weight at—minimum 5 lbs., maximum 10 lbs. It will be seen from this that there are two Pekingese Clubs in England at the present time, both in a very flourishing condition with a long roll of members. Personally I have always deprecated the breeding of very tiny specimens at the cost of type and stamina, but in the case of the " Palace Dog " we had all we desired in these points, and I therefore consider the encouragement given to the larger and coarser dog unnecessary, and in judging I should always give the preference to the good small dog ; however, I am not in accord with rigid minimum and maximum weight limits (weight should be given merely as a guide), as a heavy boned small dog in good condition will often weigh considerably more than a light boned dog in poor condition, though much larger in appearance. Type is the essential point, and should count before anything else. Pekingese are hardy, faithful, full of pluck and very active. Their fascinating ways and old-fashioned peculiarities endear them to all. They are easy to breed and rear, as may be judged from the enormous increase both in England and in the United States during the last few years, and there is still an ever increasing demand for puppies.

PEKINGESE.

Description of the Breed.

We now come to the description of the proper type of these quaint little dogs, and I may say at once that this is a subject over which there has been considerable controversy. The most debated point is one of size, and it looked at one time not far distant as if the breed might be split up into two sections, with a division by weight (in the same way as has been lately done in Pomeranians) and each given a distant name. This is advocated by Lady Algernon Gordon Lennox, with the suggestion that the one should be called " The Pekin Palace Dog " and the other

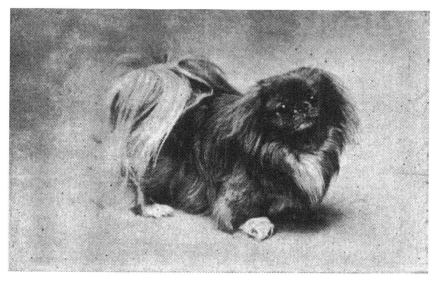

Ch. Chu-êrh of Alderbourne.

" The Pekin Spaniel " ; but I think that this would cause considerable confusion, as it is more than likely that dogs of each kind would emanate from the same litter. The breed is essentially a toy one, and there is no doubt that small ones can be bred true to type, and that it is not, on this account, necessary to encourage the larger specimens. If they have become so numerous that classes should be provided for them, by all means provide them, but do not let it be thought that a big dog is the correct thing, a really typical small dog is ten times more difficult to breed than a typical big one, and for this reason more

9

Two Lovely Prize-Winning Pekingese.

ASHTON-MORE KO-KO.
(By Kwai-Kwai of Egham ex Ashton-More Vi-Vi.)
Owned by Miss Gainsford.

ASHTON-MORE KOU-KOU.
(Litter brother to above.)
Owned by Mrs. Cecil Chandless, Sherrington Manor, Berwick, Sussex.

The Up-to-Date Pekingese.

CH. KOTZU OF BURDEROP.

SUTHERLAND OUEN-TEU TANG.

scarce. In judging I should always give preference to the smaller specimen. I do not like, as I explained in the previous chapter, a hard and fast weight limit, as a small dog with good bone and in good condition will often weigh more than a much larger one not possessing these advantages, but without doubt a certain number of points should be given for the correct size, namely, somewhere between 7 and 9 lbs., provided type, bone, and substance are not sacrificed.

The Pekingese must have a broad head, flat and wide between the ears, and not at all domed or apple-headed ; his eyes must be large, dark, and lustrous, very prominent and set wide apart, his muzzle short, broad, well cushioned up and wrinkled, and on no account pinched. These dogs should have a quaint grotesque expression peculiar to themselves and not what might be termed a " pretty " face at all. A small light eye utterly spoils the expression, and should not be tolerated. Much importance is now attached to a flat face, and broad powerful underjaw, and (according to our present standard) the mouth should be quite level ; however, as it is almost impossible to get a strong underjaw and very short face, with a *perfectly level mouth*, it would seem as if a slightly undershot mouth should be allowed, and I think it is high time we altered our standard. The slightly undershot mouth greatly improved the foreface and finish of this dog, so long as the teeth do not show. The nose should be jet black, and very broad and flat ; a light-coloured nose carries a severe penalty. The ears, in a good specimen, are long and fully feathered, and round the neck there is a bushy mane or frill. The legs, which are one of the chief characteristics of these dogs, are short and heavy, with as much bone as possible ; they are well bowed out at elbows, and profusely feathered. The feet are flat, and covered with long hair, which should increase their apparent length considerably. The chest should be broad and deep, and the body short, heavy in front, and falling away in the loins like that of a Lion, or in other words tapering to a decided " waist " behind the ribs. A well-feathered tail, carried high and turned up over the back, is a *sine quâ non*. The coat should be abundant, with long thick hair, which must be soft to the touch, and on no account curly, but a sort of double coat like that of the Collie, *i.e.*, a long straight outer, and a thick under coat ; the hair on thighs and legs should be particularly long. " The petticoats " on some good specimens measuring 6 to 8 inches in length.

With regard to colour, I may say that all are allowable, and we find a great variety of shades among the best dogs on the bench. There are reds, blacks, black and tans, fawn, biscuit, chinchilla, sable, and

CH. NANKING WENTI.

NANKING FO.

many variously shaded parti-colours, but I think that the most popular colour is a rich, golden chestnut, such as we find in most of the Good-wood strain. Sometimes the dogs are whole coloured, sometimes they have white on chest or paws, and as we know white markings are no detriment. In China the most valued colour is a golden fawn, and dogs of that shade are called " Sun Dogs," owing to their glimmering, sunshiny appearance ; the nearer they approach the Imperial yellow the better. In the Far East an all white specimen would also be thought exceedingly rare, which the following quotation from an old article of mine will prove :—" The Chinese Minister was greatly struck with a very curious pure white Pekingese, which belonged to the well-known fancier Mrs. McEwen, and said that in Pekin so great a rarity would be guarded with the utmost vigilance, and would only be allowed to take exercise within the sacred precincts of the Palace grounds, in care of at least two attendants, who would be answerable for its safety with their lives." As to markings, it is desirable that in parti-coloured dogs each colour should be distinct and clearly defined. In the whole coloured specimens a black muzzle is almost indispensable. There should be black spectacles round the eyes, also black points to the ears. A variety known as liver coloured dogs are not recognised. The feathering on tail and thighs may be of a slightly lighter shade than the rest of the body. The description given below is taken from the "Twentieth Century Dog," and said to be the words of Her Imperial Majesty Tsze-Hsi, Dowager Empress of China. It has often been quoted, and being so very apropos and quaint, will stand endless repetition :—

" Let the Lion dog be small ; let it wear the swelling cape of dignity round its neck ; let it display the billowing standard of pomp above its neck.

" Let its face be black ; let its forefront be shaggy ; let its forehead be straight and low, like unto the brow of an Imperial harmony boxer.

" Let its eyes be large and luminous ; let its ears be set like the sail of a war junk ; let its nose be like that of the monkey god of the Hindoos

" Let its body be shaped like that of a hunting Lion spying for its prey.

" Let its forelegs be bent, so that it shall not desire to travel far, or leave the Imperial precincts.

" Let its feet be tufted with plentiful hair, that its footfalls may be soundless ; for its standard of pomp let it rival the whisk of the Thibetan yak.

" Let it be lively, that it may afford entertainment by its gambols.

" And for its colour let it be that of a lion, a golden sable, to be carried in the sleeve of a yellow robe, or the colour of a red bear, or a black bear, or a white bear, or striped like a dragon, so that there may be dogs appropriate to every costume in the Imperial wardrobe.

" Thus shall it preserve its integrity and self-respect."

The Points of Pekingese.

1.—HEAD.—Massive, broad skull, wide and flat between the ears (not dome-shaped) ; wide between the eyes 10

2. NOSE.—Black, broad, very short and flat 5

3. EYES.—Large, dark, prominent, round, lustrous ... 5

4. STOP.—Deep 5

5. EARS.—Heart-shaped, not set too high, leather never long enough to come below the muzzle, not carried erect, but rather drooping, long feather 5

6. MUZZLE.—Very short and broad, wrinkled 5

7. SHAPE OF BODY.—Heavy in front, broad chest falling away lighter behind, lion-like, not too long in the body 10

8. LEGS.—Short, fore-legs heavy, bowed out at elbows, hind-legs lighter but firm and well shaped 5

9. FEET.—Flat, not round, should stand well up on toes, not on ankles 5

10. COAT AND FEATHER AND CONDITION.—Long, with thick undercoat, straight and flat, not curly nor wavy, rather coarse, but soft, feather on thighs, legs, tail and toes, long and profuse ... 10

11. MANE.—Profuse, extending beyond the shoulder blades, forming ruff or frill round front of neck 5

12. TAIL.—Curled and carried well up on loins, long, profuse, straight feather 10

13. SIZE.—Being a toy dog the smaller the better, provided type and points are not sacrificed. When divided by weight, classes should be over 10lbs. and under 10lbs. 5

14. COLOUR.—All colours are allowable, red, fawn, black, black-and-tan, sable, brindle, white and parti-coloured, black masks, and spectacles round eyes with lines to ears are desirable ... 5

15. ACTION.—Free, strong and high, crossing the feet or throwing them out in running should not take off marks. Weakness of joints should be penalised 10

                Total 100

Before closing this chapter I should like to point out to those who are thinking of taking up the breed the absolute necessity of purchasing first-class stock with which to found their kennel. Mediocre puppies

Ch. Yen Chu of Newnham.

are unsaleable, while really good ones always command their price, so if success is desired it is essential to purchase well-bred typical brood matrons. It is not everyone who can afford to buy a stud dog (as a good sire will often run into three figures), so it is advisable to send to the best dog your purse will allow. The fees for these vary from 5 to 25 guineas. From this it will be seen that the breeding of Pekingese can be a very expensive " hobby." However, there is no doubt but that it can be made to pay well too, but the great thing to remember is to start with only a few, and to have them very good. The competition in this breed is enormous, and success does not always come quickly.

I remember how very disheartened I was during the first four years I was interested in Pekingese, and I had all but given up hope of ever breeding a " flyer." However, my luck turned with the purchase of (the now well-known sire and winner) Kwai-Kwai of Egham, and from that day to this I have never had cause to regret my adoption of the breed. Little Kwai-Kwai has proved invaluable to me as the head of my kennel, and his exquisite type is now reproduced in several of its inmates. From the beginning I have bred from medium sized (not to say in many cases large) brood matrons, mated to small typical dogs, and I advise others to do the same. In Pekes, as in many other big-headed breeds, the brood bitch should be a fair size.

I might also mention here that in grooming Pekes a comb should seldom be used, and *never* on his body. It will only tear out the much prized undercoat, and thus utterly spoil the dog's appearance. My Pekes all have tremendous coats, plumes and long ear fringes, and I never use anything for them but a pneumatic pad brush made with hair bristles. This takes the place of a comb and does not destroy the undercoat at all, but if properly used encourages the growth of hair to a wonderful extent.

Ch. Lyncroft Chops.

C

APPROPRIATE NAMES FOR PEKINGESÉ.

CHUN-KO-LIANG— *A Noted General.*
CHU-JEN—*The Master.*
CHE-JEN—*Wise Man.*
CH'IEN-CHIN-SE—*Pale Gold.*
CHIN-HUA—*Golden Flame.*
CHIN-PAO—*Golden Treasure.*
CHIN— *A Pearl.*
CHIN-TAN—*Dawn.*
CHOO-TSZE— *A Philosopher.*
CHIP-PEH— *A Singing Girl.*
DOA-WHA—*Peach Blossom.*
PAI-CHUEH—*One White Foot.*
FO—*Buddah.*
FAN-TAO— *A Fabulous Fruit.*
FENG-HUANG—*Phoeniz.*
FUH—*Bat (Emblem of Happiness).*
FOBY— *Adam.*
GAI-GAI—*Clever One.*
HOO-MUM—*Tigers Gate.*
HOTY— *An Ancient Empress.*
HOONG-KIN— *Yellow Cap.*
HUNG-CHIN—*Red Gold.*
HUO-HUNG—*Flame Red.*
HIEN-TSU— *Illustrous Sire.*
HUN-TAN—*Sunrise.*
HSIUNG—*Elder Brother.*
HSUAN-NU—*The Dark Maiden.*
HU-SHIH— *A Queen Regent.*
HEI-JU-YRH—*Black as Night.*
WRI-CHU-TZU—*Black Pearl.*
KUAN-YIN— *A Goddess.*
KWAN-TI—*God of War.*
KWA-KIUM—*Solitary Prince.*
KAO-HUAN— *A Famous Statesman.*
KU-ERH—*Orphan Boy.*
KU-NEE—*Orphan Girl.*
KU-CHI—*Of Ancient Family.*

KWAI-WHA—*Little Lady.*
KYLIN— *A Sacred Animal.*
LO— *A Lily.*
LAO-TSZE——*The Old Infant.*
LANG—*Wolf.*
MEILING— *A Flower.*
MAI-MAI—*Little Sister.*
MEI-HE HUNG TAN—*Black as Coal.*
NU-YING—*Brave Lady.*
PAO-PEY—*Darling.*
PIMG-PI—*Clever.*
POO-TO— *A God.*
PAN-FEI— *A Famous Beauty.*
SHOH-DEE—*Little Brother.*
SHAMUN— *A Buddist Priest.*
SING-TSAR—*Conqueror.*
SO-PAI-CHE—*The Adored One.*
SHING-JIN— *A Sage.*
SHOU—*Longevity.*
SING SUH HAI—*Starry Sea.*
TU-SHENG TZU—*Only Child.*
TSIN-WANG—*Prince of the Blood.*
TAI-PAN—*Head Man.*
TSING-HAI— *Azure Sea.*
TI— *Younger Brother.*
TSYNG-SHIH— *Imperial Class.*
TSMA—*Old name for China.*
TAI-YUN—*Excellency.*
TIEN-HOW—*Queen of Heaven.*
YAOW-JIN—*Dog Man.*
YAOW—*Dog.*
YAO NIANG—*Deep Eyes.*
YIN-HSING—*Silver Star.*
YEN-JU-HU—*Eyes like Lakes.*
YANG—*The Sun (male).*
YING—*The Moon (female).*
WOUGH—*King.*

THE JAPANESE.

These beautiful little dogs, as their name implies, hail from the land of Chrysanthemums and sunshine, and like their short-faced prototypes the King Charles Spaniel and Pekingese, trace their descent far into the dim past, and share with them the distinction of having been Court favourites in their own country for many centuries. The Japanese people have for a great length of time bred very small specimens appropriate for carrying in the sleeves of their flowing garments,

Ch. Susuhi.

or for holding curled under the chin. These mites are called Nanoya, sleeve or chin dogs, and are usually the most sought after in their native land. However, fashion in Japan is just as capricious as it is in England, for sometimes the diminutive " sleeve " specimens are " de règle," and sometimes the larger dog. The origin of these quaint and fascinating little dogs is unfortunately a point upon which we have no authentic information. Some authorities assert that the Jap is equally indigenous to the Northern part of China ; others that they are off-shoots from the short-faced spaniels of Thibet. Pekin has also been mentioned as their possible birthplace. At any rate the little Jap has for many centuries been highly prized by the elite of their sunny island, and at the time when the feudal nobles and their fighting retainers ruled Japan each great house owned its own particular strain, which was carefully guarded in its purity and no intermingling with other strains allowed. The care of these tiny creatures fell to the little noble ladies, by whom they were greatly cherished and petted. They lived in wonderful bamboo cages as if they had been doves, and so from century to century retained their purity of strain and family likeness ; but the time came when the feudal nobles were dethroned, and their little dogs, which had been guarded so long and carefully, were scattered broadcast through the length and breadth of their native land.   And so it is that we find so many separate and distinct types in Japan.   The Jap is essentially a dainty toy, and I think that for this reason the smaller we can breed them the better, provided that type and character are never lost sight of.   We all know the great difficulty experienced in producing really diminutive specimens which are true to type and perfectly sound in all respects, and it would therefore seem only right that in the show ring such a dog should take precedence of the larger stamp, other points and condition being equal.   In England we now have weight classes (under and over 7lbs.) which gives all sizes an even chance, and greatly simplifies matters for the Judge.   With regard to breeding, the very tiny specimens though teeming with quality, have not got the constitutions of the medium sized dog, and for this reason I do not think it advisable to breed to very minute ones.   Stamina is a quality in which the race is sadly lacking, and therefore strength, which will usually accompany the larger sire, is an absolute essential if the progeny are to be fitted to withstand the innumerable troubles to which most puppies are heir. These remarks apply to an even greater extent to the brood matron, for, in addition to other advantages, it will usually be found that a small bitch has one or two large puppies, while the larger one (possibly from 6 to 8 lbs.) has a more numerous family of smaller ones, and being bred from sturdy parents the puppies will be sturdy too.   When first brought into the world they need considerable warmth, and should live in a room of an equal temperature of 60 degrees.   When they are old enough to run about they should never be allowed out on damp or cold days, but encouraged to play out in the sun on warm ones.   They must not, however, be treated as hot-house plants, and as they grow older should be got accustomed to a cooler room and more out-door exercise. A verandah enclosed in glass is a great boon to anyone possessing a kennel of Japs, in fact it is almost a necessity in a cold, changeable climate.   The windows should be made to slide up and down, so that on fine days they can be thrown wide open, allowing in all the pure air possible, and if the wind is chilly they can be kept closed, the little dogs still getting the full benefit of the sun's rays.   There is no dog which loves the sunshine as do these quaint little Orientals ; they simply revel in its warmth, and it is most amusing to watch their mad gambols,

The late Ch. ANDERSON MANOR SUME.
(Winner of 12 Championships).

Ch. ANDERSON MANOR HOKUSAN.

Imported by Mrs. Gordon-Greatrex, and considered now the best of his breed in England.

His services are at a fee of **6 Guineas.**

Apply Miss Coplin (Kennel Maid), Kennels, Clewer Park, Clewer, near Windsor.

for when thoroughly happy they are the wildest-spirited little creatures imaginable.

Japs are particularly susceptible to distemper, and seem to stand no chance against it at all, but simply succumb without a struggle. I have known kennel after kennel completely demolished by this fell disease, and it is surely the greatest danger which Japanese breeders and exhibitors have to guard against. Personally, I believe firmly in inoculation, and have had ample proof of its great value (see chapter on Distemper). English and American bred Japs are much stronger and possessed of more stamina than native bred dogs, but some of the best English strains are now becoming frightfully inbred owing to the difficulty in importing new blood, and this should be guarded against, as the Jap is such a constitutionally delicate little chap that we must not do anything to make him more so. There are not many fanciers who will import dogs from the East owing to the strict quarantine law and the fact that very few of them survive their term of detention. Japanese are extremely sensitive little creatures, and when taken away from their sunny island many of them droop and pine away, and I should think that quite one-half of the dogs which leave Japan never reach their destination at all. No wonder they are very scarce and very valuable. American-bred Japs would stand a far better chance in this respect, however, and I think it would be well worth while for English fanciers to import from America, where I have seen many specimens quite as good as anything on the English bench.

Japs require very special feeding, and their menu should be constantly changed. In their own country they live principally on rice ; but this is all wrong according to our European ideas, and I will venture to say that a meat-fed puppy will be twice as sturdy as one brought up on rice. I am a tremendous believer in meat as a staple food for dogs. Finely minced chicken, lamb or beef I consider indispensable for at least one meal a day, and I find that the best way to give it is mixed with bread-crumbs ; dry wheat biscuit is also very good, also fresh fish, plain or rolled in toast-crumbs. A little well-boiled rice may be given to them occasionally, but not much milk or dog biscuits. I mention this here as I think that the food for Japs requires to be rather differently prepared, and given in smaller quantities, than that of the average toy dog. They need very little exercise, and are usually quite content with scampering about within the garden limits. They can be the merriest, liveliest and sauciest little creatures in the world ; they are capable of great affection, and I have often noticed that people who have once owned them scarcely ever give them up. They have naturally most

Mrs. SAMUEL SMITH'S HOME BRED JAPANESE, at Coniston,
Reddington Road, Hampstead, N.W.

Ch. ORIENTAL YO-SEN.

MICHI-MONI.

cleanly habits, and have a quaint way of cleaning their faces with their paws after eating, just as a cat would do. As regards type, the most popular is the long-haired dog familiar to all show goers. He may be black and white, red and white, or lemon and white. The markings should be well distributed over a white body and over cheeks and ears, with an even white blaze running up the forehead to the top of skull. The blaze is supposed to look like the body of a butterfly with his wings represented by the long fringed ears. The head should be large in proportion to the size of the dog, the skull broad and slightly rounded, eyes large, dark and prominent, and set wide apart, ears V-shaped, placed rather high on the head and carried well forward. A point much to be desired is a broad short well turned up muzzle, with good width of underjaw and even finish ; the face as short as possible ; a compact body supported by fine well-feathered legs, in conjunction with a really good coat, and full well-carried plume, adds greatly to the grace and symmetry of the dog. The hair should be straight and silky in texture, very abundant, particularly about the throat, where it forms a ruffle. The absolute necessity of sound limbs and free movement goes without saying.

Points of the Japanese.

30 GENERAL APPEARANCE.—That of a lively, highly-bred little dog with dainty appearance, smart, compact carriage and profuse coat. These dogs should be essentially stylish in movement, lifting the feet high when in motion, carrying the tail (which is heavily feathered) proudly curved or plumed over the back. In size they vary considerably, but the smaller they are the better, provided type and quality are not sacrificed. When divided by weight, classes should be for under and over 7 lbs.

BODY.—Should be squarely and compactly built, wide in chest, " cobby " in shape. The length of the dog's body should be about its height.

15 COAT.—The coat should be long, profuse, and straight, free from curl or wave, and not too flat ; it should have a tendency to stand out, more particularly at the frill, with profuse feathering on the tail and thighs.

10 COLOUR.—The dogs should be either black and white or red and white, i.e., parti-coloured. The term red includes all shades of sable, brindle, lemon, and orange, but the brighter and

clearer the red, the better. The white should be clear white, and the colour, whether black or red, should be evenly distributed patches over the body, cheeks, and ears.

30 HEAD.—Should be large for size of dog, with broad skull, rounded in front ; eyes large, dark, set far apart ; muzzle very short and wide and well cushioned, *i.e.*, the upper lips rounded on each side of nostrils, which should be large and black, except in the case of red and white dogs, when a brown coloured nose is as common as a black one.

5 EARS.—Should be small, set wide apart, and high on the dog's head, and carried slightly forward, V-shaped.

10 LEGS AND FEET—The legs should be straight and the bone fine ; the feet should be long and hare-shaped. The legs should be well feathered to the feet on the front legs and to the thighs behind. The feet should also be feathered.

100

Ch. Atsuta.

TOY SPANIELS.

The origin of the Toy Spaniel has given rise to much discussion, and many theories have been put forward as regards it, such breeds as the Pug, Maltese, Pekingese, Jap., and even the Bull-dog having been given credit for a share in his ancestry. There is little foundation for any of these however (though it is probable that a cross has been used to obtain the present short-faced specimens), and it seems quite sufficient to note that we first make his acquaintance as a distinct breed late in the 16th Century, and that he was held in high favour some time before the restoration of the Stuarts. His first appearance in history

The late Ch. Laureate (King Charles Spaniel).

is at the death of Mary Queen of Scots, where it is related that a small black and white Spaniel belonging to the unfortunate Queen was found huddled away in the folds of her gown after her execution. Since the time of " Ye Merrie Monarch" after whom they were christened, they have been closely associated with Royalty and the favourite of many a crowned head. It was, however, in the reign of James II. that they reached the zenith of their popularity. The King himself was quite daft about his little pets, and was seldom seen without a small pack of these pampered toys. They pervaded the Royal apartments, Banquet Hall, and Council Chamber, and became so fashionable that no cortege was considered fully equipped without one or more of these soft-coated little creatures to add to the air of dainty elegance so characteristic of these days. On the fall of the Stuarts large numbers of these beloved little companions followed their masters into exile, and their presence was no longer tolerated at Court. Some of the more powerful houses, however, kept up the breed at their country seats, and they eventually recovered their Court favour and have kept it ever since. Queen Victoria was very fond of them, and the little King Charles "Dash" was one of her greatest pets and the constant plaything of the Royal babies at Windsor. He is to be seen in the arms of the young Prince of Wales in a famous portrait of the Queen and her children.

We still see the Toy Spaniel at home both in castle and cottage, and it would surprise many owners to hear that numbers of really good specimens are to be found in some of the poorest parts of London. They have also been made familiar to us in prose and in verse, while such distinguished artists as Watteau, Vandyke, Frith, Stubbs, and Landseer have immortalised them on canvas, enabling us to trace the history of the breed and to gain an accurate idea of the type and colour in vogue at the time these artists flourished. An interesting old record which bears upon the point of colour was lately unearthed in the British Museum. It advertised the loss of a Toy Spaniel nearly 200 years ago, and runs : " Whereas a little black and white spaniel bitch of King Charles breed, about six months old (the white on her neck has been lately burned) broke loose out of Mr. Nash's shop in Bishopsgate Street on Thursday last about eight o'clock in the morning, with a piece of red worsted garter about her neck. Whoever has taken up the bitch and will bring her to the Sign of The St. Martin in York Buildings, shall have 5s. reward for their pains."

The show specimen of to-day has wandered far from the original type. The latter were stout, cobby little fellows with long faces, rather flat skulls, and, according to old prints and paintings, most profuse and beautiful coats. In type they greatly resembled a small Cocker, and in the Sportman's Repository for 1820 we read that these " delicate and small carpet spaniels have excellent noses, and will hunt truly and pleasantly, but are neither fit for a long day nor for a thorny cover." I myself once owned a Blenheim who often accompanied our shooting parties and retrieved perfectly. The original Toy Spaniels were probably black and white, then the red and whites and the black-and-tans became known, and lastly the Rubys, which are a comparatively recent innovation. In their early history the dogs were all called King Charles Spaniels, but later it became the fashion

THE ASHTON-MORE TOY SPANIELS.

Ch. DARNALL KITTY.

Ch. ASHTON PERFECTION.

ASHTON-MORE PERFECTION.

ASHTON-MORE SHEILA.

Formerly owned by Mrs. Raymond Mallock, 2, Preston Park Avenue, Brighton

THE ASHTON-MORE TOY SPANIELS.

ASHTON-MORE SHEILA and ASHTON-MORE ADONIS.

SOME PROMISING KING CHARLES PUPPIES,
Bred by Mrs. Raymond Mallock, 2, Preston Park Avenue, Brighton.

THE ASHTON-MORE TOY SPANIELS.

The late Ch. ROLLO and ASHTON DEFENDER.

Owned by Mrs. Raymond Mallock

ASHTON-MORE LITTLE ROLLO.   **ASHTON-MORE TURQUOISE.**

The property of Mrs. Raymond Mallock, 2, Preston Park Avenue,
Brighton.

THE ASHTON-MORE TOY SPANIELS.

Ch. ASHTON-MORE BARONET.

ASHTON-MORE ROLLA.

Winner of 25 Championships and sire of Ashton-More Cardinal.

Ch. ASHTON-MORE CARDINAL.
Property of Mrs. Raymond Mallock, 2, Preston Park Avenue, Brighton.

among the Nobility to keep their own particular strains, those of the Howards and Churchills being the most celebrated. The latter obtained the distinctive name of Blenheim Spaniel, given to them after the Battle of Blenheim, where, so the legend goes, one of these little animals remained at the side of the Duke of Marlborough throughout the engagement, after which proof of devotion he was taken on all the Duke's subsequent campaigns, and shared with him the honours of his triumphant return. In memory of this episode the Duchess (the

The late Ch. Royal Rip (Ruby Spaniel).

famous Sarah Churchill) adopted the little Spaniel as her favourite breed. Descendants of the same strain are found in Oxfordshire up to the present day, but they are little known or appreciated away from their own home, and although some efforts were made not long ago to revive an interest in them by putting on classes at various shows for Old Type " or Marlborough Blenheims," these were badly supported, and it was found that the more modern product with his retroussè nose and bulging forehead, had too firmly established himself in public favour to admit of a rival. The breed has been known for centuries as King Charles and Blenheim Spaniels, but on the formation of the Toy Spaniel Club in 1885 the colours were still further sub-divided into King Charles (black-and-tan), Ruby (red), Prince Charles (tri-colour), and Blenheim (red and white). This nomenclature was also adopted in the States, but owing to the fact that I won a very valuable Challenge Cup for the best brace, any breed, with my Blenheim Ch. Rollo, and my Tricolour Ch. Darnall Kitty, and that the win was pro-tested on the ground that they were two different breeds, the American Kennel Club ruled that as long as the varieties were given distinct names, they must be considered distinct breeds, and therefore as this was obviously absurd, they re-classified them all as English Toy Spaniels, and divided them by colour only. The English Kennel Club also changed their nomenclature, classifying all the varieties as Toy Spaniels, but retaining the name King Charles for the black-and-tan, and Blenheim for the red and white, the Ruby and Prince Charles having to be content with a colour designation. I consider it a pity if it was necessary to give them a collective name that the name King Charles Spaniel was not adopted for the whole breed. It is historically correct, and the present title of Toy Spaniel might mean anything. Turning to the dogs themselves. The King Charles should be a deep black, with rich mahogany tan markings over eyes, on muzzle, cheeks, and legs, and lining the ears. Too much tan splashed about the face is undesirable, whilst white hairs should handicap, and a white patch disqualify the dog in the Judging ring. In most cases we find this variety with the heaviest coats, and the shortest faces. The Ruby seldom grow such profuse coats, though they share the good head properties of the above. They should be a rich deep red. Common failings are light eye rims, and lightish nose, which ought to severely penalise a show specimen. This colour is the rarest of all, and really good Rubys, either in England or America, could be numbered on the fingers of one's hand. This scarcity militates against them in such ways as the selection of a sire, and much increases the breeder's difficulty, but on the other hand makes them more sought after and more valuable. The Tricolours are great coat growers, and to my mind, when compactly built and well broken in colour, are the handsomest of all. In the Blenheim variety clear rich markings have always been easy to obtain, but the " beauty spot," I am sorry to see, is getting rarer and rarer each year, and I think that we breeders should make an effort to restore it. It is a point peculiar to this variety, and one which in bygone years was much sought after and admired. With regard to interbreeding. The orthodox method is to cross King Charles with Ruby, and Blenheim with Tricolour. In the first case the advantages gained by this alliance

D

SOME OF Mrs. RAYMOND MALLOCK'S OLD FAVOURITES.

TWO HANDSOME KING CHARLES SPANIELS.

BUNTY.

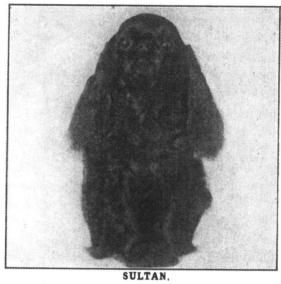

SULTAN.

Owned and bred by Mrs. Neville-Williams, The Cottage, Riverfield Road, Staines

TWO NOTED AMERICAN TOY SPANIELS.

UNIQUE WEE.   Ch. ROYAL QUEENIE.

Ch. THE ADVOCATE.

THE FAMOUS TRICOLOUR TOY SPANIELS.

Ch. ZANA.

Ch. GOLD WAVE.

Owned and bred by—
Mrs. POTTER, 4, Cross Oak Road, Berkhampstead.

are to the King Charles brighter tan, and to the Ruby richer colour, the chance of white minimised, and the length of coat and feathering increased. The occasional use of the Blenheim is necessary in breeding Tricolours, in order to improve the tan markings, which are otherwise liable to totally disappear, and also to counteract a tendency to heavy markings, which detracts so much from their beauty. *Vice versa* Tricolour blood is required for the Blenheims for the sake of richness of colour, and for the better head properties they seem to produce owing to the Tricolour being more closely allied to the short-faced black-and-tans. If Blenheim is bred to Blenheim for several generations, the red

The late Ch. Dannall Wild (Tricolour).

markings deteriorate into a washy tan, the eyes and nose become light, and the animals grow plainer in face, and their skull less domed, reverting in time to the Old Marlborough type. Another method of breeding the broken colours is to go direct to the King Charles. Many of our best dogs have been bred this way, and although you must be prepared for one generation of badly-marked specimens, in the next generation (Blenheim blood being again introduced) the progeny should be correctly marked with great gain as to head properties and general quality. This method I have found the shortest road to success, but it requires a thorough knowledge of individual dogs in the pedigrees

TENGA.

ROSIE'S ROSEBUD.
The property of Mrs. Rollo Stewart, 17, Kingsburgh Road, Murrayfield, Edinburgh.

39

which is difficult for the novice to arrive at, and therefore must be left to the more advanced breeders.   Speaking generally, the present day show specimen is not particularly easy to breed and rear (though the average puppy gives little or no trouble).   I think that constant in-breeding and the craze for small absolutely noseless specimens has done much to reduce the stamina of this breed.   It must be remembered that it is the fancier's weakness to run to extremes, and by the time a "halt" is called much harm has usually been done.   A medium-sized dog is what we want, and do let us try to breed them with well-balanced bodies, profuse coats, and sound action.   The movement of Toy Spaniels in the show ring at the present time is notoriously bad, and it is a very great pity that it should be so.   Good head properties are of

The late Clevedon Wallie (Tricolour).

course very important, but *compact* little figures and free action are of equal moment, and we must combine them all in the ideal dog.   Exag-gerations of any kind are to be condemned, such as a protruding under jaw.   This is very often found in the so-called noseless dogs, but it is an ugly fault, and gives a monkey-like finish to the face which quite spoils the expression.   The wonderful dignity of the old-time spaniel with his deep chest and massive head, is quickly disappearing, and one seldom meets with the typical mincing gait which belonged to the best dogs of some 20 years ago.   I have often wished that one could see many of their good points restored, and I am quite sure that if fanciers go on breeding an exaggerated type and forget the bodies which carry their wonderful heads, that the Toy Spaniel will lose all of his remaining charm.   There is not a Blenheim on the bench to-day to compare with my dear old favourite the late Ch. Rollo ; he weighed 12 lbs., and looked a small dog. He was not nearly so short in face as many of the present day champions, but his muzzle was broad and beautifully cushioned up, his legs short and sturdy, and his figure and action simply ideal. He has left his stamp upon his descendants, and I only hope that his wonderful figure and sound movement may continue the strong features of his line. The Toy Spaniel will be found by all who know him to be a gentle and affectionate little pet. Having been an aristocrat of aristocrats for many generations, good manners are innate in him, his bearing in the house is full of self possession, and although very intelligent and full of fun, he is seldom noisy or obtrusive. The combination of these characteristics render him an altogether desirable little friend and companion.

In England, the original Toy Spaniel Club (founded in 1885) is still flourishing and continues to foster and encourage the breed. In the States there is also The Toy Spaniel Club of America, of which I had the honour to be the Founder.

The following is the revised Standard drawn up by the Toy Spaniel Club in 1913, and also an old standard for Marlborough Blenheims, which is not mentioned in our Club Book.

Points of the Toy Spaniel.

10. SKULL.—Massive in comparison to size, well domed, and full over the eyes.

10. EYES.—Very large and dark, set wide apart, with eyelids block square to face line, and with pleasing expression.

10. NOSE.—Black with large wide open nostrils, very short, and turned up to meet skull. The stop between skull and nose should be well defined.

10. JAW.—Muzzle square, wide, and deep, and well turned up, lower jaw wide, lips exactly meeting, giving a nice finish. The cheeks should not fall away under the eyes, but be well cushioned up. A protruding tongue is objectionable, but does not disqualify.

10. EARS.—Set on low, and to hang quite flat to cheeks, very long and well feathered.

5. SIZE.—The most desirable size is from 6 to 12 lbs.

15. SHAPE.—Compact and cobby, on refined lines, chest wide and deep, legs short and straight, back short and level. Tail well flagged and not carried over the level of back.

15. MOVEMENT.—Free, active, and elegant.

10. COAT.—Long, silky, and straight, a slight wave allowed, not curly. The legs, ears and tail should be profusely feathered.

5. COLOUR.—*King Charles* : A rich glossy black, with bright mahogany tan markings on muzzle, legs, chest, lining of ears, under tail, and spots over eyes.

Tricolour : A ground of pearly white with well distributed black patches, brilliant tan markings on cheeks, lining of ears, under tail, and spots over the eyes. A wide white blaze between the eyes and up the forehead.

Blenheim : A ground of pearly white with well distributed chestnut red patches. A wide clear blaze with the "spot" in centre of skull. (A clear chestnut red mark about the size of a sixpence in the centre of skull).

Ruby : Whole coloured. A rich chestnut red.

100

DISQUALIFICATION.—The presence of a few white hairs on the chest of a Black and Tan or Ruby is undesirable, but a white patch shall disqualify.

The late Ch. Red Lancer,
Winner for best Toy Spaniel in Show every time shown.

Ch. Bayard (Tricolour Toy Spaniel).

The late Ch. Rococo (King Charles Spaniel).

43

GRIFFON BRUXELLOIS.

The origin of this quaint little dog is not far to seek, but very far to find, and perhaps it is wiser to take him as he is, and to leave his somewhat doubtful ancestors in a halo of oblivion. Suffice it to say that he has now become a very distinct type, especially so in England, where more care has been bestowed on his breeding and development than in his native land, where a good deal is left to chance.

Copthorne Troubadour.

Of all toys he is the only one in which the coat should be harsh and rough, and on this account possesses an advantage over most breeds, as he is able, without detriment to it, to accompany his owner in walks and scrambles over rough country, and is altogether one of the sturdiest, brightest and most generally useful and companionable little fellows that I know of.

His chief characteristics are, a large head, short undershot jaw, full black eyes, bristling whiskers, rough red coat, and cobby body. He should have the "Tête de Singe" and the more monkeyish in expression the better he is. In Brussels his ears are always cropped, and this adds greatly to his smartness, and gives him an alertness of expression which is sometimes lost when his ears are left " au naturel," as they have to be if he is to win on the English bench.

His name is somewhat misleading, as it is really only an adjective meaning that his hair should be of the texture of the Griffon, and it is by no means confined to this breed ; several other rough-coated dogs,

PAULA D'ECOSSE.

MASABAN D'ECOSSE.
The property of Mrs. ROLLO STEWART, 17, Kingsburgh Road,
Murrayfield, Edinburgh.

45

such as Griffon Bassetts, having the same appellation. It is rather an anomaly, too, that classes have been made for smooth-coated Griffons, a combination which is obviously impossible, therefore it is a pity that some more distinctive name, such as that used in France (where they are known as Brussels terriers), was not given to this breed ; but Griffon is short and convenient, and, moreover, suits the little dog, and once given is likely to remain.

As regards breeding it must be borne in mind that the Griffon's origin is of recent date, and therefore great care must be exercised in selecting well-authenticated stock,—a task which is by no means easy, if you are looking for it in their native land, as the records of their parents are short and often inaccurate, and the breeder who is not very careful is apt to get surprising results, by the pups harking back to their not very distant and cosmopolitan ancestors. Inbreeding, too, must be carefully guarded against, as it soon destroys their stamina and intelligence, the latter characteristic being among the most charming of these little monkey-dogs, and without which, however true to type, they are but sorry copies of their true selves. As regards size, it must be remembered that as with other breeds it is not the smallest bitches which produce the smallest pups, and that a bitch of fair size, say about eight pounds, and a small but strong dog would probably be the best combination. As with Toy Spaniels, the size of their head makes the breeding of them more difficult than that of most other toy breeds.

Griffons in England are making steady progress. In fact, so popular have they become that a third Club was formed shortly before the War to look after the interests of the "Any other Colour than Red," which is getting to be a very strong section of this variety. The blacks have improved wonderfully, and now have well-filled classes at our shows, and at last the Kennel Club has granted Challenge Certificates for the Brabacons (smooths). The improvement in type and general character is ever on the increase, and a " soft coat " from which many a good dog suffered in the past, would never be tolerated now in the show ring. I am glad to see that the craze for diminutive specimens has not yet spread to this breed, and I feel sure that we have to thank several of our foremost breeders for their sound common sense in averting this danger. The Griffon was never intended to be extremely minute, and the best dogs of to-day, as far as I remember, are very little smaller than the original ones.

In America the first strong class was shown at the Toy Spaniel Club's Show in 1905. Since then many beautiful dogs have been exported from England, and the breed is making splendid progress.

It is obvious that the little Griffon is going to attract a lot of attention, and that on his merits is sure to be more and more sought after and admired.

Points of the Griffon Bruxellois.

GENERAL APPEARANCE.—A lady's little dog, intelligent, sprightly, robust, of compact appearance, reminding one of a cob, and captivating the attention by a quasi-human expression.

HEAD.—Rounded, furnished with somewhat hard, irregular hairs, longer round the eyes, on the nose and cheeks.

EARS.—Semi-erect.

EYES.—Very large, black, or nearly black, eyelids edged with black, eyelashes long and black, eyebrows covered with hairs, leaving the eye they encircle perfectly uncovered.

NOSE.—Always black, short, surrounded with hair converging upwards and going to meet those which surround the eyes ; very pronounced stop or break.

LIPS.—Edged with black, furnished with moustache : a little black in the moustache not a fault.

CHIN.—Prominent, without showing the teeth, and edged with a small beard.

CHEST.—Rather wide and deep.

LEGS.—As straight as possible, of medium length.

TAIL.—Erect, and cut to two-thirds.

COLOUR.—Red.

TEXTURE OF COAT.—Harsh, wiry, irregular, rather long and thick.

WEIGHT.—Light weight, five pounds maximum, and heavy weight, nine pounds maximum.

Kennel-maid with some of Mrs. Raymond Mallock's
Toy Spaniel brood bitches.

POMERANIANS.

There are few more popular Toy breeds in existence than the perky
" Pom," and on looking back over the past few years one cannot help
being impressed by the rapid strides he has made in popularity, and by
the vast changes which have taken place in the breed. In order to
correctly point out these changes it will be necessary to go back a little
and speak of the dog's origin and condition when we first made his
acquaintance. There seems to be little doubt but what he originally
hailed from Pomerania, though, unfortunately, we have no record of

Ch. The Sable Mite.

when he was first introduced into our country. We read of him, however, in the Sportsman's Cabinet (at the beginning of last century), in
rather uncomplimentary language, as being a "noisy, snappish,
frivolous little tyke, and dangerous with children." Noisy he still is,
and frivolous, but such faults have now become virtues, and the noisy,
perky, saucy " Pom " is one of the most petted and pampered canines
of the present era. He has been known and recognised under a wonderful category of names, viz., Loup-Loup Pomeranians, Wolf Dog,
Volpino, and Spitz, under which name for many years he lived and
flourished in our land. But it was not until quite recently that he

TWO CELEBRATED POMERANIANS.

Ch. HOME FARM SABLE ALEN.

Ch. MUCH MORE.

became so popular as a house pet, for the Spitz was a much larger dog, twenty pounds or so in weight, and he appears to have been an ill-tempered and quarrelsome fellow with few friends and many enemies. It would seem improbable that the present-day Pomeranians, with their sweet dispositions, diminutive forms, and wonderful variety of colour, should all have sprung from the same stock, and yet we have no proof that other blood was introduced. Very little was known of the Pom in England prior to 1871, when the Kennel Club recognised the breed, and they made their first appearance on our bench. For some years following their progress was slow, and it was not until a Club was formed some twenty years later that a real impetus was given to the breed.

The first dogs we hear of were of a pale yellow colour ; they were rather long in body, but very fox-like in head, expression, and movement, and they eventually became extinct. The Spitz made his debut on our show bench as a pure white animal, though the tinge of yellow about the ears of a white specimen (which is now counted a grave fault) leads to the impression that in all probability he was descended from the old yellow variety. Later on, black and other coloured dogs were imported from Germany. They were much smaller than our own white ones, and so began the breeding of toy Poms. Year after year the size has been decreased, and beautiful new varieties of colours produced, till now we see the Pom the acme of perfection,—truly a convincing proof of the breeder's skill. The Pomeranian exhibit is to-day one of the most important features of the great English shows, where classes are provided for dogs under and over seven pounds in weight, and for a variety of colours. White specimens, for a long time somewhat unpopular, and certainly the most difficult variety in which to breed good, small ones, now appear to be coming in vogue again, though I do not believe they will ever be so popular as the browns, blacks, blues, or charming little shaded sables. These latter are now quite the latest fad, and long prices may easily be obtained for good small ones. A bright, rich orange (though rare) is much sought after, and the parti-colour, a comparatively recent innovation, is, when gaily marked, very pretty and attractive.

In speaking of individual dogs the shaded sable Ch. Ruffle was my first love ; I only made his acquaintance when he was an old dog, but I quite lost my heart to him, and very soon after I became an enthusiastic breeder and exhibitor. Of my own dogs I shall only mention the late Champion Ashton Merry Scamp, and I think that he is worthy of notice, as he was, without doubt, one of the best browns ever seen on the American bench, and a Champion many times over.

In America few Poms are exhibited in really full coat, which is partly due to the climate, but principally to the fact that they are kept too warm, and that furnace heat (which, alas! is used in many kennels) is ruinous to a healthy growth of hair. These dogs have such heavy coats that they do not require much heat to keep them comfortable, and if treated like hothouse plants will certainly never develop that profusion and quality of hair so universally admired. They should be seldom washed, as there is nothing more injurious to the coat than too many baths, whilst careful and proper grooming will keep the hair in good condition. For quite a number of years the standard of points of the Pomeranian remained practically unchanged, but recently it was deemed necessary to revise them owing to the enormous advance made in breeding, and of their division into Pomeranian and Pomeranian Miniatures. I cannot do better than quote this new standard, for it goes most thoroughly into all details. The difficulty in producing Miniatures possessing the beautiful wedge-shaped head of the larger specimens, has only been overcome by careful and scientific breeding, but they can now hold their own in this and all other respects, and an apple-headed Pom is no longer tolerated.

Scale of Points of the Pomeranian and Pomeranian Miniature as adopted by the Pomeranian Club in 1909.

APPEARANCE.—The Pomeranian in build and appearance should be a compact, short-coupled dog, well knit in frame. He should exhibit great intelligence in his expression, activity, and buoyancy in his deportment. ...　...　...　...　...　... 10

HEAD AND NOSE.—The head and nose should be foxy in outline, or wedge-shaped, the skull being slightly flat, large in proportion to the muzzle, which should finish rather fine, and be free from lippiness. The teeth should be level, and should on no account be undershot. The hair on the head and face should be smooth and short-coated. The nose should be black in white, orange, and shaded-sable dogs ; but in other colours may be " self-coloured," but never parti-coloured or white　...　...　...　...　... 10

EARS.—The ears should be small, not set too far apart, not too low down, but carried perfectly erect like those of a fox, and, like the head, should be covered with short, soft hair　...　...　... 5

EYES.—The eyes should be medium in size, not full nor set too wide apart, bright and dark in colour, and showing great intelligence. In white, orange, shaded-sable, and cream dogs, the rims round the eyes should be black　...　...　...　...　... 5

NECK AND BODY.—The neck should be rather short and well set in. The back must be short, and the body compact, being well ribbed up and the barrel well rounded. The chest must be fairly deep and not too wide, but in proportion to the size of the dog   ...   15

LEGS.—The forelegs must be well feathered and perfectly straight, of medium length, and not such as would be termed "leggy" or "low on leg," but in length and strength in due proportion to a well-balanced frame. The shoulders should be clean and well laid back. The hind legs and thighs must be well feathered down to the hocks, and must be neither "cow-hocked" nor wide behind. They must be fine in bone and free in action. The feet should be small and compact in shape   10

TAIL.—The tail is one of the characteristics of the breed, and should be turned over the back and carried flat and straight, being profusely covered with long, harsh, spreading hair...   5

COAT.—There should be two coats—an undercoat and an overcoat ; the one, a soft fluffy undercoat, the other, a long perfectly straight coat, harsh in texture and covering the whole of the body, being very abundant round the neck and forepart of the shoulders and chest, where it should form a frill of profuse, standing-off straight hair, extending over the shoulders. The hindquarters should be clad with long hair or feathering from the top of the rump to the hock   25

COLOUR.—All whole-colours are admissible, but they should be free from white shadings. At present the whole-coloured dogs are :—White, Black, Brown (light or dark), Blue (as pale as possible), Orange (which should be deep and even in colour), Beaver, Cream (which should have black noses and black rims around the eyes).   Whites must be quite free from lemon or any other colour. A few white hairs in any of the self-coloured dogs shall not necessarily disqualify.   Dogs other than white with white or tan markings are decidedly objectionable, and should be discouraged. They cannot compete as whole-coloured specimens.   In particoloured dogs the colours should be evenly distributed on the body in patches ; a dog with white or tan feet or chest would not be a parti-coloured dog. Shaded-sables should be shaded throughout with three or more colours, the hair to be as uniformly shaded as possible, and with no patches of self-colour. In mixed classes, where whole-coloured and parti-coloured Pomeranians compete together, the preference should, if in other points they are equal, be given to the whole-coloured specimens   15
                                                                                    100

ITALIAN GREYHOUNDS.

These charming little dogs, the very acme of grace and beauty, once so popular, seem to have lost in public favour of late years, though I am glad to say that there are still left several staunch supporters of the breed who are taking care of its interests and breeding animals as true to the Italian standard as has been done in past years. No doubt this toy's fragile appearance and general delicacy has had much to do with its present lack of popularity, still they are not so frail as their slender proportions would lead one to imagine. They usually are very

Queen of the South, Sussex Queen, Princess, Cream and Sunny King.

jolly little things, and will take keen delight in a run on a fine day, and even in winter, if carefully blanketed, derive much amusement and exercise by chasing the sparrows or anything harmless which happens to come their way.

They are a breed of great antiquity, and have been kept in England as far back as the seventeenth century, enjoying the royal favour of many a Sovereign, while, in Prussia, the famous Frederick the Great simply idolised them, and even left instructions in his will that his body should be buried among his pets in the Greyhound cemetery, in the Park of Sans Souci. Lately there has been considerable discussion as to their correct colour, but the standard recognises all shades of fawn, mouse, white and red, all others being considered off-colours, and not of much use for exhibition purposes. It is, however, interesting to note that the old-time dogs were found in a variety of shades, for at Hampton Court, in a painting of the Queen of James I., there are several grey-hounds, including fawns, blues, and blue and white, showing that as far back as those days a variety of colours existed. Even up to a few years ago pure whites and blue were in favour. The original Italian seems to have been a much larger dog than is now in vogue, and weighed in the neighbourhood of fourteen pounds, while the present-day specimens must not exceed seven and one-half pounds, and the smaller they are the better. Reducing their size has also greatly reduced their stamina, and the inbreeding found in most pure-bred dogs does not tend to improve their constitutions. Great difficulty is experienced in produc-ing very small yet typical animals without impairing their health, and, unfortunately, a toy terrier cross is sometimes used, which, though it has the effect of producing diminutiveness, brings serious defects, notably the bulging eye and the apple head, both of which are most difficult to eradicate. In appearance the Italian greyhound should resemble his "cousin of the leash," in miniature, though built on more fragile lines, less muscular and somewhat slimmer in form. In point of elegance he stands alone, being an exquisitely modelled little creature, whose every movement indicates grace personified, while the peculiar prancing action is a distinct characteristic of his own. Tulip, or prick ears, are bad faults and should be studiously avoided, likewise a compactly built or well-ribbed-up body, as it shows the terrier cross. Further evidence of terrier blood may be found in the puppies when first born, which will usually be black-and-tan, while in pure bred animals they are whole-coloured, or possibly fawn-and-white. In disposition the Italian is gentle and affectionate, and not really half so delicate as his fragile form would suggest. In cold weather he requires to be kept in the house, and should have a comfortable basket (free from draughts) to sleep in, and when taken out for a "run" in winter-time must always be blanketed.

Italians can, as a rule, stand a good deal of exercise, which is almost essential if they are to be kept in good condition, and great care should be taken not to overfeed them, as these dogs must not be allowed to grow fat if they are to retain the beautiful lines of their graceful form. A writer at the beginning of the 19th century alludes to them as "diminutive native breed, which seems only calculated to soothe beauty and indulge frivolities. These dogs are so deficient in spirit, sagacity, fortitude and the self-defences of every other sort of the canine race as not to be able to officiate in the service of domestic alarm and protection, and in consequence are dedicated only to the comforts of the tea table, the fireside carpet, the luxurious indulgences of the sofa, and the warm lap of the mistress." This seems rather rough on the poor little greyhounds, and certainly not true of the present-day animals, for they are sharp watch-dogs and can hear the slightest sound. It is true that they still know how to enjoy the fireside carpet, and can make themselves quite warm and " comfy " among the soft cushions of the sofa, but they can likewise take keen delight in a scamper over the lawn, and are quite as capable of enjoying a healthy life as any of the numerous varieties of toy dogs.

Standard.

GENERAL APPEARANCE.—A miniature English greyhound, more slender in all proportions, and of ideal elegance and grace of shape, symmetry and action.

HEAD.—Skull flat, long and narrow ; muzzle very fine, nose dark in colour, ears rose-shaped placed well back, soft and delicate, and should touch or nearly so behind the head ; eyes rather large, bright and full of expression.

BODY.—Neck long and gracefully arched ; shoulders long and sloping, chest and brisket deep and narrow, back covered and drooping at the hind quarters ; loin well arched and cut up.

LEGS AND FEET.—Fore-legs straight, well set under the shoulders, fine pasterns, small delicate bones ; hind-legs, hocks well let down, thighs muscular, feet the long "Hare's foot," with arched toes and well slit up.

TAIL, COAT AND COLOUR.—Tail rather long, fine with low carriage. Coat skin fine and supple, hair thin and glossy like satin ; colour, preferably self-coloured ; the colour most prized is golden fawn, but all shades of fawn, red, mouse, blue, cream and white are recognised, and blacks, brindles, and pied are considered less desirable.

ACTION.—High stepping and free.

WEIGHT.—Two classes, one of eight pounds and under, and one over eight pounds.

THE YORKSHIRE TERRIER.

Notwithstanding recent innovations and " fashionable fads " for other canine pets, the dainty little Yorkshire Terrier still ranks a prime favourite. He well deserves his place, for a more intelligent, bright, and generally attractive little chap it would be difficult to find in the doggy world. In tracing the origin of the Yorkshire it will be necessary to go back to the days when he was known as broken-haired terrier, and killed rats on a Sunday morning. Some authorities state that he

The late Ashton Premier. Owned by the Authoress of this book.

was first brought into Yorkshire and Lancashire by Paisley weavers, and certain it is that in many respects he resembles the Glasgow or Paisley Skye ; but I am inclined to believe that the broken-haired terriers known some sixty years ago in the West of Yorkshire, notably at Bradford and Huddersfield, were the ancestors of our present breed. They were bright, game little tykes, weighing from ten to twenty pounds, black-and-tans, with longish rough hair, and strong punishing jaws, which they used to some purpose in the plebeian occupation of rat killing, at which sport they became famous. Even to this day (in spite of well-oiled and long sweeping coats), they retain their sporting instincts.

Up to this period there seems to have been no definite object in breeding, beyond the desire to get a sound, game little terrier, and by pure accident a softer-coated dog became known. It probably was at this time that the blood of the Paisley Skye was introduced, and the long soft coats began to be cultivated. Some years later a new breed sprang to life in the vicinity of Leeds, probably a cross between the Maltese and the wire-haired Fox-terrier, resembling the latter in body and conformation, and the former in length of coat, which was of a light silver shade. These dogs were known as "silver" terriers, and were greatly admired for their wonderful wealth of coat, and became most popular when classes were provided for them at the leading shows. In the course of time they were crossed with the strain previously mentioned, with the result that the progeny showed a certain amount of golden-tan on head and legs, and body colour of a silvery blue, and so it was that the Yorkshire Terrier became an established and recognised breed. The first dog of any note was the now famous Huddersfield Ben. He was owned by Mr. and Mrs. Foster, of Bradford, and extensively shown by them. He proved a great winner, and also a great sire, and may truthfully be called the "father" of the breed. I regret more than I can say having lost his photo, which was given me by Mrs. Foster shortly before she died. It was greatly prized by me, and historically interesting as well, for it contained on its back a list of the dog's winnings, which now does not appear to be known. The coat of the Yorkshire has year by year been wonderfully developed by careful treatment, his size gradually reduced and colour improved, and we see him to-day a masterpiece of the breeder's skill. He is truly a most beautiful "toy," with his great wealth of long silken tresses, his bright little face, and small, keen eyes ever on the watch for fun of any sort. As a pet and companion I know of few dogs to take the place of the Yorkshire. He is exceedingly intelligent, as "bright as a button," a sharp little watch-dog, and brimful of pluck. Many of the modern dogs display a wonderful amount of sporting instincts, which no doubt they inherit from their yeoman ancestors. A good Yorkshire does not know the meaning of fear, and it is not an uncommon sight to see one of these small game things tackle an enemy four times his size. Many of them are also great ratters, and I regret to say that my first Yorkshire, "Racket," a dainty little creature, and one of the best I ever owned, was much given to this unladylike sport. She was often badly bitten, but it never seemed to dampen her courage, and even when she grew old (she lived to sixteen) I had the greatest difficulty in keeping her small ladyship out of trouble. I have several of old Racket's great, great, great, great, grand-children with me now, making seven generations I have bred of the same strain.

Yorkshires are unusually healthy little dogs, with wonderful constitutions, and any amount of stamina ; they are very easy to breed and rear, and not so difficult to get in nice coat as one would imagine, though abnormally long coats can only be grown under the eye of an expert. Personally, I am opposed to the extreme coats, as it necessitates an artificial treatment, which is most unnatural, and injurious to the dog's general health and happiness, and makes the little creature unfit for a pet or the merry little companion he can be when not so hampered. A certain amount of coat is very attractive and quite proper, and can readily be grown. I have found the following preparation most excellent for promoting the growth : Six ounces of Neatsfoot oil, six drachms of tincture of cantharides, six drops of oil of rosemary. This should be carefully rubbed on the skin, then the coat brushed one way, so as to work the oil thoroughly through the hair. One pound of cocoanut oil, a half-pound of vaseline, and one ounce of paraffin well mixed together is another very good dressing, and should be applied as above, and about every three days. Many people do not like to oil their little house pets, and for them I should recommend Pinaud's Eau de Quinine, a sweet-smelling tonic and wonderful hair grower. I use gallons of it every year for my dogs, and think that their splendid coats bear testimony of its value.

The grooming of a Yorkshire is an all-important matter, and much of his general appearance depends upon how this is done. The hair should be divided from the nose to the tip of the tail in an even parting, and be brushed straight down on each side, using one of the special long-bristled brushes which most dog-furnishing shops can supply. If the " fall " is very long, it had best be plaited and tied on top of the dog's head, and his feet should be kept in small bags (made of calico) to prevent his sharp little claws catching in his hair and tearing it out. One " tub " a fortnight is usually sufficient, as much washing is most injurious to the hair, and as regards soap I advise the preparation known as " Sunlight " soap. It is extensively used in England for long-haired dogs, and in my own kennel it and Shirley's Shampoo are used exclusively. On washing a Yorkshire prepare a tub one-fourth full of warm soap suds, place him in it and wash very carefully, taking care not to tangle his coat. When he is clean, rinse him thoroughly in lukewarm water, removing every atom of soap, then wrap him in a soft towel and pat him gently, so as to absorb the greater part of the water still remaining, but do not ruffle his hair or rub it the wrong way. The dry brush should then be brought into requisition, and the process of grooming continued until he is quite dry. It is advisable to use several brushes, as they get wet after a time, the last and polishing brush being somewhat softer than the others.

It is not necessary to put anything on a Yorkshire's coat to make it shine with the exception of well-directed " elbow grease "; for it is the brushing after the coat is dry that brings out the natural oil, and produces a beautiful glossy appearance. I always spend at least an hour in washing and grooming a Yorkshire for exhibition, so my readers may imagine that it was no light task to show a team of these little creatures, as I have done many times. Occasionally a novice will slightly grease his dog before taking it into the ring, with the idea that it makes the coat look more glossy, but this is a most unwise thing to do, and if detected will disqualify his exhibit. So much depends upon the condition in which the dog is put down, that it really takes an experienced person to prepare him for shows, and to manipulate his coat while in the ring.

A show Yorkshire should not weigh over six pounds, and I consider four-and-a-half pounds the ideal size in a show or stud dog. Many of the " midgets " will be found lacking in head properties, a point most essential to the preservation of the true characteristics of the breed. The large dogs for the most part carry the best coats, though often the small ones will be found of sounder colour. Personally, I confess a weakness for the beautiful even steel blue, and richness of tan over great length of coat, and am glad to see that such an important point is at last being given its due in the judging ring. It is not " a lot of hair with a dog attached " that we want, but a sound, compactly built and level-backed little fellow, with a moderately long coat, rich golden tan on head and legs, and a sound and even-coloured " blue " back. My own preference is for a real " terrier " head, but a great many people nowadays prefer a shorter, so to speak, prettier face. The eyes should be small and expression very bright, and good action is, of course, a *sine quâ non*. With regard to breeding (as in most toy varieties) it is a great mistake to breed from small bitches. Rather select a typical well-bred and sound-coloured brood matron, capable of growing plenty of coat. A bitch from six to eight pounds is the best size, and I should advise the beginner to procure a " reliable breeder," one that has had puppies before, and has proved herself a good mother. This will, of course, apply to any breed, and is really a most essential point in purchasing stock for breeding purposes. It is a peculiar fact that the puppies are black and short-haired when born, and that as they grow older the colour changes. Many a novice has been greatly perturbed on finding the brood bitch nursing a litter of these little darkies, and a story is told of a now prominent exhibitor who had all his first puppies drowned, saying that they were black-and-tan mongrels. The little ones will be found sturdy and easy to rear when compared with most other toy breeds, and very fascinating they can be to their owners. I remember very well my delight over my first Yorkshire puppies, what really interesting and funny little chaps they were, with their gray-bearded faces making them look like so many little wizened old men. They would play and frolic by the hour, were up to all sorts of pranks, chasing butterflies round and round the flower beds or anything and everything which came in their way, but nothing seemed to please these young scamps so much as pulling their unfortunate mother about by the ears, or by tearing out long tufts of her hair, and nearly choking as they attempted to swallow it. They were, indeed, a joy to me, and ever since has the Yorkshire held a very big place in my heart.

Points of the Yorkshire Terrier.

GENERAL APPEARANCE.—The general appearance should be that of a long-coated pet dog, the coat hanging quite straight and evenly down each side, a parting extending from the nose to the end of the tail ; the animal should be very compact and neat, the carriage being very sprightly, bearing an important air ; although the frame is hidden beneath a mantle of hair, the general outline should be such as to suggest the existence of a vigorous and well-proportioned body.

HEAD.—Should be rather small and flat, not too prominent or round in the skull, rather broad at the muzzle, a perfectly black nose, the hair on the muzzle very long, which should be a rich deep tan, *not* sooty or grey, under the chin long hair, and about the same colour as the centre of the head, which should be a bright golden tan, and not on any account intermingled with dark or sooty hairs. Hair on the sides of the head should be very long, a few shades deeper tan than the centre of the head, especially about the ear roots.

EYES.—Medium in size, dark in colour, having a sharp intelligent expression, and placed so as to look directly forward ; they should not be prominent. The edges of the eye-lids should also be a dark colour.

EARS.—Preferred, quite erect ; if not, to be small V-shaped and carried semi-erect, covered with short hair ; colour to be deep dark tan.

MOUTH.—Good even mouth, teeth as sound as possible, a dog having lost a tooth or two through accident not the least objectionable, providing the jaws are even.

BODY.—Very compact, good loin, level on the top of the back.

COAT AND COLOUR.—The hair as long and as straight as possible (*not wavy*) which should be glossy like silk (not woolly) ; colour a bright steel blue, extending from the back of the head to the root of the tail, and on no account intermingled with fawn, light, or dark hairs.

LEGS.—Quite straight, which should be of a bright golden tan, and well covered with hair a few shades lighter at the ends than at the roots.

FEET.—As round as possible ; toe nails black.

TAIL.—Cut to a medium length with plenty of hair on, darker blue in colour than the rest of the body, especially at the end of the tail, and carried a little higher than the level of the back.

Scale of Points.

Quantity and colour of hair	25	Mouth	...	5
Quality of Coat	15	Ears	...	5
Tan	15	Legs and Feet ...	...	5
Head	10	Body and appearance ...		10
Eyes	5	Tail	...	5
		Total	...	100

THE FAMOUS PEKINGESE.

Ch. Yenny Westlecott.

TOY TERRIERS.

" Toy Terrier," as the name implies, includes numerous varieties of diminutive terriers, which usually weigh under seven pounds according to the standard laid down for each particular breed. Owing to the meagre entries of these little creatures at our shows (Yorkshire and Maltese do not come under the category) the classification is somewhat restricted for their variety ; but a fancier specially interested in any particular variety can quite easily secure separate classification for it by guaranteeing the sufficient number of entries. It is surprising how often one meets people who do not know of this rule, which is a capital one, as it gives exhibitors the chance to open new classes, which the show

The Toy Terrier, Champion Coquette.

committee do not feel justified in doing on account of the poor entries of that breed during the past. When, however, the necessary number of entries is guaranteed at a few shows, and classes fill fairly well, the show people (always ready to encourage exhibitors) will on their own account give classes for that particular variety, and if they are well patronised, the success of the breed is assured. The bench show committee is largely influenced by the entries at its former show. Where a breed has filled remarkably well, new classes are added, and where it has been but poorly represented they are cut, therefore exhibitors must make entries if they are to keep their dogs before the public. To return to the Toy Terriers themselves ; among them are the old favourite black and tans, which reigned supreme for so many years. Of late they have rather had their noses put out of joint by the livelier toy bull-terriers ; in fact, so popular have these latter become of late that I hear rumours ot a club being formed to look after their interests. The Toy Bull-terrier should be a miniature of the larger breed, and perfectly white in colour, any small patches of brindle or yellow being undesirable, though, unfortunately, they appear in many otherwise excellent specimens. As in most varieties where a breed has been tremendously reduced in size, a really typical specimen is most difficult to obtain, the average usually being too short in face and too round in skull, and with faulty jaw formation. I have seen them as small as two and-a-half pounds, but the majority are considerably larger, and more true to type. In disposition they are kind and affectionate, and real gamy little tykes, with great big hearts in their small bodies. They do not know the meaning of fear, and, always on the alert for sport, will, without a moment's hesitation, challenge foes ten times their size and weight.

There has been a gradual falling off in the good old toy black-and-tan terrier of recent years, though the breed still holds on. In this variety possibly more than others, the apple head and goggle eyes are too much in evidence, and especially in the very diminutive atom of dog flesh. They should be counterparts of the Manchester terrier, any approach to the Italian Greyhound type being most objectionable. In head properties the very small ones usually fail, and I have seldom seen one weighing much less than seven pounds with a really typical good head. The colour should be black and tan with plenty of tan of a bright rich shade, and on the tan each toe should be clearly pencilled with a thin line of black determining at the knee, also distinct thumb marks, and the tan spot on each cheek small and clearly defined. In tail, they differ slightly from their larger cousin, the Manchester terrier, whose caudal appendage is long and commonly known as a " whip-tail," while a desideratum in the toy variety is the three-quarter length tail. This is a distinctive point between the two breeds, and fanciers should not lose sight of the importance of it, neither should they fail to pay proper attention to the coat, which must be like silk to the touch, and not velvety. These seem minor points in themselves, but in reality are most important ones.

In breeding black and tans it is a common mistake to breed from very small, and therefore imperfect specimens, and in such cases the logical result would be apple-headed and undesirable progeny. The right road to success is to breed direct from the Manchester. It takes time and patience, as a rule, to follow this course, but it is the only way

to get the approved-of type, and dogs of a sound and hardy constitution.   Diminutiveness is all very well in a Toy, but not to the
exclusion of type, and exhibitors should bear this fact in mind when
their wonder of " two pounds " is beaten in the show ring by a typical
dog which is just able to squeeze into the class for " Miniatures,"
for it is symmetry, type, and general appearance the Judge is looking
for, not smallness at any cost.

There are several other Terriers which come under this heading,
namely, the Smooth White Terrier (which should be without a speck of
any other colour), the Blue and Fawn, and several other kinds of long-
haired specimens.   These, however, are very rare and are rapidly
becoming extinct, a larger and more robust type of dog taking their
place.   The Toy varieties are judged by the same standards as are
used for the larger breeds.

In England the word " Miniature " is used for the "Lightweights,"
and in the States they are known as " Toy " so and so.

Mrs. E. C. WALLACE'S PEKINGESE.

Ashton-More Tendwa.

THE SCHIPPERKE.

In the Schipperke we have a quaint little tailless canine, who since his importation from Holland some twenty-two years ago has made for himself so many friends that he is now counted in England as one of the most popular dogs, and well he deserves such title, for a more intelligent small chap it would be difficult to discover anywhere. In his native land he is found on the Dutch canal boats, where he fills the post of watchman and companion to the bargemen, from whose occupation he derives his name. He is a splendid swimmer, and to kill rats is the delight of his life ; he is as quick as a wink, and always on the alert. He should be born " without a narrative," but it occasionally occurs that a puppy will appear with his caudal appendage intact, in which case the surgeon's knife is called into requisition to remove the offending

Ch. Percy.   Ch. Peabody.

member, and so skilfully can this operation be performed that even the eyes of an expert will be unable to detect it. In England, black is the acknowledged colour, while in Holland a dark fawn-coloured variety is equally popular. As regards weight the Belgium Club divides them into two classes, one nine to twelve pounds, and one twelve to twenty pounds, while with us twelve pounds is about the maximum, many of our best being considerably under that weight. To my mind the smaller ones are preferable and make most engaging little companions, as well as capital house dogs. Being blessed with a hardy constitution they can go out in the worst weather, and will take as much fun out of a run across country and chase as many rabbits as any terrier. Then, too, they have the sterling qualification of faithfulness, which, coupled with their natural instinct as watch-dogs, makes them altogether most taking " doggies " and useful ones to boot.

The following, which appeared in "Chasse et Peche " in 1885, is so interesting and so truly characteristic of the Schip that I think it is well worth reproduction .

" The Schipperke, or bargee's little dog. A little devil, black all over, but without the cloven foot and minus a tail ; such is the bargee's dog. A veritable demon after rats, mice, moles, and anything he comes across. A tireless guard, he takes rest neither day nor night, and is always on the alert. Alive to all that is going on inside or outside the house, he allows nothing to escape his attention from the cellar to the garret, and should he remark anything amiss he acquaints his master of the fact in piercing barks. He knows the way of the house, interferes in everything going, and finishes by persuading himself that it is he who directs the whole. His fidelity to his master is unalterable, his kindness to the children more than tried, but ill-luck to the stranger who has the rashness to lay his hand on anything or anybody. The Schipperke has teeth, and knows how to use them.

" One often meets him on the barges of the canals and rivers of Flanders. He does not make the deck dirty, or upset the things upon it with his tail—for the very good reason that he hasn't one.

" A good stable dog, he is the great chum of the horses, and has an excellent seat. His joy is to mount the towing-horse ; it is then that he struts and barks at the passer-by ; he would like to make them believe that it is he alone who gets the boat along."

Standard.

HEAD.—Foxy in type. Skull should not be round but broad and with little stop. Muzzle moderate in length, fine but not weak, and well filled out under the eyes. Nose black and small ; eyes dark brown, small, more round than oval, and not full ; bright and full of expression Teeth strong and level.

EARS.—Shape : Of moderate length, not too broad at base, tapering to a point. Carriage : Stiffly erect, and when in that position the inside edge to form as near as possible a right angle with the skull, and strong enough not to be bent otherwise than lengthwise.

NECK.—Strong, full and rather short, set broad on the shoulders and stiffly arched.

SHOULDERS.—Muscular and sloping, chest broad and deep in brisket, back short, straight and strong, with loins powerful and well drawn up from the brisket.

LEGS AND FEET.—Fore-legs perfectly straight, well under the body, with bone in proportion to the body. Hind legs strong, muscular, with

.hocks well let down. Feet small, catlike and standing well on its toes ; nails black

HIND QUARTERS.—Fine compared to the fore part. Muscular and well-developed thighs, tailless, and rump well rounded.

COAT.—Black, abundant, dense and harsh, smooth on the head ears, and legs, lying close on the back and sides, but erect and thick round the neck, forming a mane and frill, and well feathered on back of thighs.

WEIGHT.—About twelve pounds.

GENERAL APPEARANCE.—A small cobby animal with sharp expression, intensely lively, presenting the appearance of being always on the alert.

DISQUALIFYING POINTS.—Drop or semi-erect ears.

FAULTS.—White hairs are objected to, but are not disqualifying.

Scale of Points.

Head, Nose, Eyes, Teeth	20	Hind-legs	5
Ears	10	Feet	5
Neck, Shoulders, Chest...	10	Hind-quarters ...	10
Back, Loins	5	Coat and Colours ...	20
Fore-legs	5	General Appearance	10
		Total	100

THE FAMOUS PEKINGESE.

Ch. Phantom of Ashcroft.

PUGS,

The points of the Pug have changed but little during the past twenty years, though the average specimen that one sees now is of sounder colour and more typical than he was some years back. They undoubtedly are a very old breed, but from whence they sprang can only be surmised, as authorities differ so in their opinions. Some affirm that Pugs were brought from Holland many years ago, having been originally imported thence from the Cape of Good Hope, and later brought over to England. Others claim they first came from Muscovy, and many writers state that they were a cross between the English Bulldog and small Dane.

In point of fact they were not heard of in England till about the time of William III., after whose accession they became great favourites

The Black Pug, Black Fairy.   The Fawn Pug, Ch. Loki.

among the aristocracy, and were generally pampered and petted to their heart's content. They were also supposed to have been most popular at the Dutch Court about this time. The great painter Hogarth has immortalized this breed in many of his most famous pictures, thus proving their great popularity in the Flemish provinces during his lifetime.

In England they continued to flourish, sometimes in and sometimes out of fashion, and between the years 1840 and 1850 the strains known as the " Willoughby " and " Morrison " first made their appearance. The former was named after Lady Willoughby de Eresby, an enthusiastic fancier who succeeded in obtaining a dog from Vienna, formerly the property of a Hungarian Countess. He was badly marked, a sort of smutty brindle and black, about twelve inches high, well built, but somewhat long in face. In 1864 he was mated to a bitch imported from Holland, of correct fawn colour, with black mask and trace, but without brindle. She had a shorter face and more powerful underjaw than the dog, and it was from this union that the celebrated Willoughby Pug, conspicuous for its " saddle mark " or " wide trace," found its origin. Then came the Morrison strain of richer colour and without much black marking. This is a larger type, and supposed to be a lineal descendant of the stock owned by Queen Charlotte.

From Stonehenge we learn that " the Pug derives his name from a Greek word which forms the root of the Latin *pugnus*, a fist, as his profile closely resembles a man's hand when tightly clenched. This is open to question. It is more likely to have arisen from a study of the countenance as well as general appearance of the animal. The jet black muzzle, or mask, secured for him the term " Carlin," from the resemblance to a harlequin who was famous in France during the middle of last century. Previously the breed was known in that country as " dogmus " and " roquets," names still retained in various parts. The breed was carefully propagated and highly esteemed during many years, exclusively as parlour pets, many wealthy families having their specially pure and celebrated Pugs. Such was the rage of fashion that no lady was seen abroad without her pet ; and when the owner sat for his or her portrait, that of the Pug occupied a prominent place in the foreground. The old English breed was distinguished by a black patch on the head, known as the black velvet, "but the best breeds of to-day are destitute of the mark."

With stately bearing and a great assumption of dignity, "the Pugs are unmistakably of the class of Vere de Vere," and well they know their own importance. I have found them generally very affectionate, and exceedingly jealous of any attention their mistress may bestow upon other members of the doggy community, also good tempered, placid and easy going. I am glad to say that the objectionable lolling tongue and the asthmatic snoring, so prevalent among this breed not long ago, is disappearing. It is a mistaken idea that Pugs can do with little exercise, for, of all pet dogs, they have the greatest tendency to obesity, which should be carefully guarded against if the dog is to remain in a healthy condition. Then, too, they are gross feeders and will usually ferret out anything edible that may be left lying about, so precautions should be taken that Master Pug does not appropriate more than his regular allowance of food each day. I have myself owned

and bred a number of them ; in fact, little " Topsy" was one of the first
dogs I ever owned, and was dearly beloved by me as a child.

One often hears the expression " as stupid as a Pug dog," which is
misleading, as the Pug of to-day certainly is everything but stupid ; in
fact, I can recall several remarkable instances of intelligence displayed
by this dog.   In 1886, a strain of all-black Pugs was introduced on the
English show bench.   Numerous theories as to their origin have been
expounded, the most probable one being that they were first imported
from the Far East.   Certain it is that Lady Brassey procured several of
these little black dogs during her voyage in the "Sunbeam," and there
seems every reason to believe that the subsequent crossing of these dogs
with the English breed produced the present black Pug.

Every year this breed is being improved, and is now, with the
exception of colour, a facsimile of the old fawn variety.   At first the
blacks were weak in facial properties and too high from the ground ;
but these defects were overcome, and we now have the little race of
" darkies " possessing a lovely raven black coat and with all essential
Pug characteristics.   They are judged by the same standard as the old-
fashioned fawns, and only differ as to colour, which should be a jet
black, any brownish or rusty shadings being most undesirable, a white
patch almost fatal.

Standard.

GENERAL APPEARANCE.—A large-headed, smooth-coated, active
and bright little dog, square built and cobby in shape.

SIZE AND CONDITION.—The Pug should be *multum in parvo*, but the
condensation should be shown by compactness of form, well-knit proportion, and hardness of developed muscles.

WEIGHT.—From thirteen to seventeen pounds.

BODY.—Short and cobby, chest wide, ribs well sprung.

LEGS.—Strong, straight, of moderate length, and well under the
body.

FEET.—Neither so long as the foot of the hare, nor so round as that
of the cat, well-split-up toes, with nails that are black.

MUZZLE.—Short, square, blunt but not up-faced.

HEAD.—Large, massive and round, not apple-headed, with no
indentation of the skull.   Eyes dark in colour, very large, bold and
prominent, globular in shape, soft and solicitous in expression, very
lustrous and when excited full of fire.   Ears thin, small and soft, like
black velvet.   The button ear is preferred to the rose ear.

MARKINGS.—Clearly defined, the muzzle or mask, ears, moles on cheeks, thumbmarks or diamond on forehead and black trace should be as black as possible.

MASK.—Black, the more intense and well defined the better.

WRINKLES.—Deep and large.

TAIL.—Curled tightly over hip. A double curl is perfection.

COAT.—Fine, smooth, short, glossy, neither hard nor woolly.

COLOUR.—Silver or apricot fawn. Each should be very decided, so as to make a contrast between colour and the trace and mask.

TRACE.—A black line extending from the occiput to the tail.

Revised Standard of Points of the Pug Dog Club.

	Fawn.	Black.		Fawn.	Black.
Symmetry	10	10	Eyes	10	10
Size	5	10	Mask	5	—
Condition	5	5	Wrinkles	5	5
Body	10	10	Tail	10	10
Legs ⎫ Feet ⎬	5	5	Trace	5	—
			Coat	5	5
Head	5	5	Colour	5	10
Muzzle	10	10		—	—
Ears	5	5	Total	100	100

THE FAMOUS PEKINGESE.

Ch. Chuty of Alderbourne.

MALTESE.

The Maltese is the most ancient breed known to Western history, his origin dating so far back that it is lost in the mists of antiquity. Aristotle speaks of them in glowing terms as early as B.C. 370, and they are also often heard of in the legends of Ancient Greece, and were considered among the most valued possessions of the Patrician dames of Rome. For centuries, too, Maltese were the Court pets of the Royal ladies of France, and many an idle hour was saved from ennui for these frivolous but charming beings by the bright playfulness of their living

Major-General Baden Powell II.

toys. Since the fall of the French monarchy they have followed its fortunes, and though now seldom found in Royal favour. there are yet a few who are still the pride and joy of their mistress' heart, and who can trace their lineage to the snowy white dogs of ancient times. Early writers have mentioned these little fellows as being indigenous to Malta, but as there were two Islands of Malta, or Melita, as they were then called, one in the Adriatic Sea, near Dalmatia, and the other in the Mediterranean, it is difficult to know to which to credit this little dog's birthplace. At all events, the Canes Melitaei of the old world appear to have closely resembled our present specimens, and the dog fanciers of the time to have been adepts at the art of breeding and rearing these beautiful little creatures. Diminutiveness was as highly prized then as it is now, and the wonderful silken tresses were of equal importance. They have been known of different colours, the red and whites being specially fashionable in the 17th century, but now only pure white specimens are recognised. In disposition the Maltese is gentle and affectionate, quick witted and full of life, and as an indoor companion of rank and beauty, the tiny fellow is peerless. " Reclining upon his cushions by the side of his fair mistress, a pure-bred Maltese looks more like a handful of brilliant white spun silk than a living creature, but pay him a little attention and he will spring to his feet, lift his fine short ears, and hasten to show you how keenly alive and alert he is from the black tip of his atom of a nose to the waving end of his snowy plume of a tail."

A good Maltese should not weigh over 6 pounds, and smaller specimens are more desirable. The coat of immaculate whiteness should be long, straight, and exceedingly silky, any tendency towards woolliness being objectionable. The nose and eyes must be black, the ears small and drooping, and quite hidden by hair, and the mouth level. A perfectly black nose is a point especially prized among fanciers, while the pale fawn coloured markings on the ears of so many otherwise excellent specimens is a severe handicap. The tail should be profusely feathered and carried over the back, and the general appearance should be that of a well-proportioned toy dog. This is one of the few Toy Breeds in which America holds the trump cards. Maltese are exceeding rare in England, and I have never seen one on the English bench to hold a candle to those exhibited in the States. The numerical points are as follows :—

Points of the Maltese.

5 HEAD.—Should not be too narrow, but should be of a Terrier shape, not too long, but not apple-headed.

5 EARS.—Should be long and well feathered, and hang close to the side of the head, the hair to be mingled with the coat at the shoulders.

5 EYES.—Should be a dark brown, with black eye rims and not too far apart.

5 NOSE.—Should be pure black.

5 LEGS AND FEET.—Legs should be short and straight, feet round, and the pads of the feet should be black.

10   BODY AND SHAPE.—Should be short and cobby, low to the ground,
        and the back should be straight from the top of the
        shoulders to the tail.

10   TAIL.—Should be well arched over the back and well feathered.

20   COAT, LENGTH AND TEXTURE.—Should be a good length, the
        longer the better, of a silky texture, not in any way
        woolly, and should be straight.

15   COLOUR.—Any self colour is admitted, but it is desirable that
        they should be pure white ; slight lemon marks should
        not disqualify.

10   CONDITION AND APPEARANCE.—Should be of a sharp terrier
        appearance with a lively action, the coat should not be
        stained, but should be well groomed.

10   SIZE.—The most approved weights should be from 4 to 9 pounds,
        the smaller the better, but it is desirable that they
—   should not exceed 10 pounds.

100

Ch. Melita Snowdream.

FEEDING.

PUPPIES.—The dieting and care of young puppies is a very important matter, and one which greatly affects their health and constitution after they have gained maturity. Great care must be taken to see that their food is always perfectly fresh, properly prepared, and that it is given in the right quantities. At four weeks I teach my puppies to lap, and also give them a small spoon to lick which has been well smeared with Virol. This is wonderful stuff for delicate puppies, and a great bone former. I unhesitatingly recommend for very young puppies a preparation known as Horlick's Malted Milk. To anyone living in town the difficulty of obtaining pure cow's milk is very great, while Horlick's Malted Milk can be procured anywhere, and made fresh whenever it is needed. It has the advantage of being about the strength of the mother's milk, while cow's milk is much weaker, and therefore should never be diluted with water and given to puppies at a time when bone-forming substance is so essential. If cow's milk is used it should be boiled, and a little cream added. Nestle's Milk is also excellent and I much prefer it to cow's milk. In the case of very small delicate puppies, I have found peptonised milk a great boon, as the pepsin aids digestion and thus saves much trouble. Peptonoids can be obtained in liquid state as well as in tablets. In the latter form they should be dissolved in milk, and are almost tasteless. Lime-water is another article which helps in the same way (for directions see Dainty Feeders and Invalids), and should be kept in all well-regulated kennels. It can readily be made by procuring some slacked lime, say a piece the size of an egg, which should be put into a quart jar, and the jar filled with clean water, corked, and allowed to stand for twenty-four hours. The water should then be poured into another jar through a piece of ine muslin, care being taken not to shake up the lime at the bottom. It is then ready for use, and the first jar may be re-filled and the same process continued until all the lime is dissolved.

As the puppies grow older it will be necessary to supplement the milk diet by adding a sponge cake, Robinson's Groats' or Freeman's Rusks, and this should be continued until they are eight weeks old. I have also found a hard boiled egg, chopped fine, and mixed with toast crumbs an excellent thing to give occasionally, especially if the puppies have any sign of diarrhoea. To the bill of fare at this point may be added two meals of finely minced cooked beef, mutton, chicken or rabbit, with gravy and brown bread (or puppy biscuits put through the mincer) mixed in. The whole to be of a crumbly consistency and on no account sloppy.

This food may be continued with the following variations until the puppies are four months old, when they can be fed as adults.

Well boiled tripe or paunch, cut into small dice, and mixed with brown bread or biscuit crumbs, a nice creamy rice or sago pudding, made with new milk, a suet pudding, or fish, from which all bones have been removed.

In addition to the above I must emphasize the fact that I consider finely minced raw beef an absolute necessity. It may be given in small quantities from the time puppies are a month old, a piece the size of a small marble may be scraped quite fine, and given once a day to a puppy four weeks old. When six weeks of age the amount may be doubled, and at three months a dessert spoonful is the correct quantity. This I give in addition to the regular food already mentioned.

No hard and fast rules can be laid down as to the amount of food to be given, as puppies, like people, require different food and in varying quantities, but regular hours should be adhered to. I give my little families five small meals a day from six weeks to three months, three from three to six months, and two from six months on, with an occasional biscuit and drink of milk thrown in.

I must also impress upon the novice the necessity of a good-sized mutton bone for the puppy when he is cutting his second teeth, which occurs when about six months of age. Puppies should be fed on nutritious food, and the best is none too good for them, and it is impossible to exercise too much care in seeing that they get proper and regular meals. They should not be kept hungry, nor be allowed to over-feed, and there must be no half-finished meals left lying about.

GROWN DOGS.—Proper feeding is one of the most important factors in keeping house dogs in good condition, and the necessity of having their meals at established intervals is of equal moment. Dogs differing in temperament and strength require different foods, and those that take an unusual amount of exercise, or are of a highly nervous disposition, will want more nourishment than is usually given to the average toy. All will enjoy a change of diet, and they should not be kept too long on any particular kind of food. Many house pets are fed not wisely but too well, with the natural result that they become old, fat and sluggish before their time, a burden to themselves and a great care to their mistress. All this can easily be avoided if the owner will take a little care in seeing that the pet has proper exercise and meals at regular hours, and is not allowed every toothsome morsel which may happen to come his way. Mid-day is the proper time for feeding when only one meal is allowed, and when two are necessary when two are necessary the principal one should be early in the day, as a heavy meal at night often results in uncleanliness. Sloppy mixtures I do not recommend unless one has some special reason for giving them, while *hot* food is most injurious to digestion, and ruinous to the teeth. Lean meat, scraps from the table mixed with brown bread-crumbs, or well-boiled rice and gravy, should form the principal diet, while about twice a week vegetables cooked and thoroughly mixed in the food will be a desirable alternative. Boiled fish (from which all bones have been removed) or boiled tripe, are agreeable accessories to the regular regime, and raw minced beef mixed dry with shreaded-wheat biscuit is usually devoured with great gusto.

Cornmeal and oatmeal, while " filling at the price," are too heating for constant use. Barley, sago and tapioca are good occasionally ; rice, too, is a capital food when mixed with other ingredients, being very easily digested and not fattening, and I strongly advise using a fair portion of it whenever practicable. Spratt's puppy cake or "Ovals" given dry, or a bone, will act as a tooth-brush, for it must be remembered that dogs' teeth should be given work to do. There is danger in small and brittle bones ; a knuckle of veal or mutton is the most desirable, while chicken, chop or steak bones should be seduously avoided. It is most important that dogs should always have access to fresh drinking water, which may be placed in bowls in convenient places. Tea they also enjoy ; it has the effect of stunting the growth if given regularly, but is otherwise harmless. With regard to dog biscuits, I use Hyde's "Yono" almost exclusively for my adult dogs, and " Rodnim " or " Viscan " for " flappers," mixed with minced meat and good broth made from calves' feet, sheep's head or ox cheek, boiled until it becomes a thick jelly.

During the war we were unable to obtain butchers' meat for our dogs, so we had to fall back on horse flesh and sheep's paunches, and it is astounding how well they fared on this very plebeian diet. My own " Pack " practically lived on paunches for two years, and were never better in their lives. It is an ideal food for dogs, being light and easy to digest and absolutely non-heating ; but paunches take a tremendous lot of cleaning, and must be cooked out of doors in a big copper on account of the smell ; otherwise, I am sure they would be more universally used. I see no objection to using the best cuts of horse flesh occasionally. My own dogs have it now three times a week, and I don't believe there is a healthier or happier lot anywhere, if I say it, who shouldn't.   Horse-meat should be well boiled before use, and never given raw.

I never fail, once a week, to give my dogs a small quantity of finely chopped well-cooked liver for medicinal reasons.   If this routine is carefully carried out the bowels will be kept in proper condition.

GROWN DOGS should be given plenty of meat.   Finely minced raw beef should always be part of their daily menu, while a new laid egg beaten up in milk is very tasty and a useful adjunct.   The dog should be fed some hours before the arrival of a visitor.

BROOD BITCH.—During pregnancy a brood bitch should be fed four times a day on nutritious and specially digestible food.   Lightly roasted chicken, or mutton, or well boiled fish, tripe or rabbit are best for her, and eggs in any form.   I also recommend my standby raw beef (a heaped up tablespoonful every day), for it is strengthening and stimulating, and both mothers and infants will thrive the better for it.

During the last week a small pinch of flax seed should be added daily to the food, also green vegetables and liver given occasionally to regulate the bowels, which must be well looked to at this time.

Horlick's Malted Milk is refreshing and especially helpful to nursing mothers, for it increases the secretion of milk and will always tempt them even when they are out of sorts.   I have yet to see a dog refuse it, especially in tablet form.   Give warm milky food *only* for three or four days after the puppies arrive and then feed up as much as possible.

A bitch requires quite three good meals a day as well as milk whilst suckling her puppies.

INVALID FOOD.—For invalids I have found Liquid Beef Peptonoids indispensable, as it contains all the good qualities of beef juice and is always ready for use, whereas the latter must be made fresh every day and takes a considerable time to prepare.   A delicate puppy, no matter how young, may be given this in small quantities with perfect safety, and I have known a dog with distemper to live on it for weeks.   It is also an excellent tonic and appetiser, and I give it in preference to anything else if a dog seems off his food. Brand's Essence of Beef and Benger's are also valuable in cases of illness, and the white of an egg is also one of the finest things you can give, especially in cases of gastritis or sickness.   Very sick dogs should be given " Vichy " water to drink or barley water ; the latter can be made by boiling a cupful of barley in a quart of water, which must, of course, be strained off, and may be mixed with peptonized milk to make it more palatable.   Horlick's Malted Milk is equally good and very fattening.   A lean piece of mutton cut from the joint, or minced chicken or rabbit, will usually tempt the most fastidious ; a baked custard is excellent ; also a hard boiled egg or well boiled paunch—the latter is the lightest and most easily digested food known ; it is even better than tripe. Paunch is merely undressed tripe, and dogs infinitely prefer it to tripe. Of course, if he will eat raw beef so much the better for him, as nothing really takes its place for a very sick dog. I fear that my readers will think I am too insistent on the subject of raw beef, but I have found it so invaluable that I want to impress upon others the necessity of using it. It can be scraped by merely scooping out the pulp of the meat with a sharp knife, and leaving all the skin and sinews behind. In this way you get the portion which is most easily digested, and the remainder can be made into beef tea. For grown dogs mincing should suffice, as the scraping process is very extravagant.

It is well to remember that in giving food to tone up a dog's system the treatment must be persevered in, for it is no use feeding a dog up one day and neglecting him the next.

WASHING AND GROOMING.

Grooming is the best method of keeping the dog's coat and skin in good order, while too much washing, especially where highly medicated soaps are used, is injurious to both. The amount of washing necessary entirely depends on the breed, for while such dogs as Maltese, Yorkshire Terriers, Japs or Blenheim Spaniels require a tub about once a fortnight, Pekingese not nearly so often, with Schips, Black Pugs and even the diminutive black-and-tan, it might almost be a semi-annual event. In the case of species where a harsh coat is desirable (such as Brussels Griffons), excessive washing is unwise, and constant and thorough brushing should take its place. When a bath is given, it is a common practice to dissolve a little borax in the water, as it has a tendency to harden the coat.

Long-haired dogs should be carefully groomed at least every second day, using a brush with very strong long bristles, while the short-coated ones may be rubbed down with a hand glove. An extra polish, given with an old silk handkerchief, adds greatly to the beautiful glossy appearance. In washing a short-haired house dog, use warm water (never hot) ; give him a thorough shampooing, applying plenty of soap, and then rinse with clean lukewarm water, to which a little bluing should be added for white animals. This should be quickly accomplished and followed by a thorough drying with a rough towel and finishing off with a good hand rubbing, which is advisable on account of its stimulating effect on the skin.   In long-coated varieties it is best not to use soap on the coat itself, but to prepare a small tub about one-third full of warm water and soap suds in which the dog can stand while you lather him well, and when he is thoroughly cleaned pour over him tepid water till every vestige of soap has disappeared. After the water has been squeezed from his coat, place him on a table and brush till he is perfectly dry (at least two brushes will be needed before his toilet is completed).   As regards soap I prefer (and use exclusively) either Shirley's Shampoo or the ordinary Sunlight preparation.

Unless it is absolutely necessary young puppies should not be bathed, but if a sponging becomes essential, it should be quickly done, and the little one carefully dried and placed in a flannel-lined basket near the fire.   Do not wash a dog for at least an hour after it has been fed, and on no account give him a swim in the sea, salt water being most injurious to the hair.   In the summer season, after a bath and a quick rub down, dogs may be allowed to run in the sun, but when it is cold or chilly they should always have their " tub " by the fire, and be kept in the house for some hours after the bath.

I can bring to mind many cases where Yorkshire Terriers and Maltese have been sent from the judging ring without a prize, simply because their owners did not know how to wash and brush them, and have seen inferior dogs put over them when beautifully groomed and shown in the pink of condition.   It requires a good deal of experience to wash and prepare either of the above varieties for exhibition, and they should be washed if possible the morning of the show.   Other breeds, such as Pekes and Poms, ought not to be " tubbed " for at least a week prior to being shown (except where, owing to their colour, it is necessary, and in such cases I advise washing the morning of the show as the coat stands out so much better when the dog has just come out of his " tub, " A thorough rubbing with hot bran and a real good brushing afterwards should be all that is necessary for the average dog in good condition before he enters the judging ring.

In grooming Poms, the coats of which should " stand out " the hair must be brushed the wrong way, and in long-haired dogs, such as Maltese and Yorkshire Terriers, it should be parted evenly from nose to tail and brushed straight down on each side.   For show specimens, if the coat is very profuse, it is advisable to tie it up and to keep the hind legs in small bags to prevent tearing the hair when scratching, and its consequent injury to a carefully-developed coat.

There are several kinds of hair dressing which are of use after washing is completed, and when brilliancy of coat is essential. Of these, Pinaud's Eau de Quinine is my favourite, as it is a delightful and sweet smelling tonic, greatly assisting the growth of the hair, and is not greasy. It should be rubbed into the skin and well brushed in after the dog is dry. Rosaline is another excellent tonic which is extensively used by many of our most successful exhibitors, and which I can also highly recommend.

It is very important to use the right sort of brush for your dog, as the different textures of coats require totally different brushes. Special brushes are made for Yorkshire Terriers, with extra long bristles placed rather wide apart in clusters; a short bristle " Dandy " brush should be used for short-coated dogs, and a pneumatic pad brush with stout hair bristles set far apart for such as Pekes, Poms, Griffons, Japs, Toy Spaniels and the like. I attach a great deal of importance to brushes and the way they are used. They assist the growth of hair immensely in the hands of an expert, but can also do a great deal of damage if too heavily used. Brushing should be lightly done with a sort of flick at the end. A comb should never be used on the body of a dog whose undercoat it is desirable to preserve. The pneumatic pad brush will take its place without the slightest damage to the undercoat.

Other points which require attention in the toilet of toy dogs are the ears and eyes. The latter should be carefully wiped and well dried every morning with medicated cotton wool, and the former cleaned at least once a week by means of a small swab of cotton rolled on the end of a match, and if there is an accumulation of wax or a dark discharge, as sometimes occurs, a few drops of Shirley's Canker Lotion dropped into the ear will soon put matters right.

EXHIBITING.

To anyone desirous of keeping dogs for profit, there is nothing which pays so well as exhibiting, and though the actual cost of showing is seldom defrayed by the prize money won, the amount of advertising you get in this way and the fact of keeping your dogs before the public are of the greatest possible benefit. After winning at several shows, your kennel will begin to get known, and your stock to command higher prices than formerly. As a start it will be necessary either to purchase a good dog or to breed him, and the next essential is to learn how to keep him in show form, so that when he enters the judging ring he will be of able to "hold his own." Condition, for which twenty-five points out

G

a possible one hundred is frequently allowed, is of the utmost importance in exhibiting, and many a champion has been turned down for lack of it.

The average well-cared-for dog (except when he is changing his coat) ought to be put in show condition with merely a little extra grooming. If, however, he had possibly been allowed to get too fat, or too thin, you must look to him, and in the event of your not being able to get him fit in time, do not run the risk of giving him a bad name by exhibiting, as many judges retain their first impression of a dog, which, if unfavourable, will take some time to eradicate. Nothing adds so greatly to the general appearance as a good coat, which, in a healthy animal should always be in the pink of condition, therefore pay special attention to the health of your dog, and all such things will come naturally. More grooming and less washing is my advice. (See previous chapter).

Making entries for a show requires some pains, and the form ought to be carefully filled out, giving name of dog, date of birth, sire and dam, and breeder, and the classes in which he is to compete. The definition of classes, with all rules, will be published in the schedule, which should be studied, as it is easy to make a mistake that will disqualify your dog should he win a prize. A common error with beginners is in not registering their dogs, which is compulsory before being shown, and also it is necessary in England to have them officially transferred by the Kennel Club if they have been registered by a former owner. This latter rule does not apply in the States. The address of the English Kennel Club is 84, Piccadilly, W., and that of the A.K.C., 221, Fourth Avenue, New York. Registration and transfer forms may be had from them on application. These preliminaries having been attended to, it will be necessary to make certain preparations for the comfort of the dog. He should have a soft cushion to lie on in his little cage, and a pretty curtain to line the inside of the pen, and an enamel saucer for water. A brush and comb, a soft towel, with which to wipe the eyes before entering the ring, a collar and a fine thin lead, comprise the entire necessary paraphernalia. I always have my " toys " benched in especially-made glass exhibition cages, and consider it the only really safe way to show valuable dogs. These cases have glass fronts, wooden sides, and wire netting on the top. Very attractive collapsable cases can now be bought at most dog furnishing shops, and I strongly advise using them. If, however, this is not done, the show pen must be well disinfected with Formalin or Lysol before the dog is put into it.

I always advise providing one's own feeding dishes and food, as the biscuits supplied by the show authorities generally upset toy dogs, and in many cases cause severe attacks of diarrhoea. Little pet dogs are often more or less off their feed at such times, due to the unusual excitement and noise, and it is best to take for them the most tempting food. Horlick's Malted Milk tablets are of great value on such occasions, as they are easily carried and all dogs delight in them.

When the eventful day arrives and you take your dog to the show, see that he is supplied with a suitable collar and lead, and that his number or tag has been securely fastened to the end of his lead (it may worry him if you fasten it on his collar), and also do not forget to bring the identification paper, which is necessary to " pass " the dog in, and must be left with the superintendent with the usual deposit if he is to be removed at night. On reaching the show, find out when your " class " is likely to be judged so that you can have your dog groomed and ready to lead into the ring when his number is called. Some dogs are naturally good showers, and literally " ask for the prize," while others are painfully shy and nervous, and remain cowering in a corner, and frequently refuse to lead. . Such poor behaviour is more or less the owner's fault, as a dog should be broken to the lead and accustomed to crowds and noise before he is exhibited, otherwise he stands little or no chance against the well-trained competitors. Some judges will take infinite pains with a nervous animal and give him every possible chance to show himself, while others will simply overlook him altogether.

You should be careful to display the dog's strong points without unduly exposing his weak ones, and to keep him as much as possible under the judge's eye. A small piece of boiled liver passed quickly over his nose will usually make him prick his ears, and look his very best, while sometimes a ball thrown along the ring will entice him to run after it, thus showing his " action." In leading a dog around a ring, encourage him to look bright and lively. When in the ring attend strictly to business ; if the judge is looking your way see that your dog is standing well, with head up and eyes bright. Do not pay attention to what people by the ringside are saying ; do not lose your temper over anything that may occur in the ring. Judges are not infallible, and there are often instances where a dog gets more than he deserves and vice-versa.

People who are unable to control their feelings in the show ring ought not to exhibit. The best evidence of sportsmanlike qualities come out in the way defeat is accepted. The " graceful loser " is admired by everyone, while the poor loser gets little sympathy, although she may cause a considerable amount of amusement. She must learn to accept the judge's decision, be it what it may. We are not bound to show under him unless we wish to do so, but having once entered and been " turned down," it is exceedingly bad form, to say the least of it, to go about casting aspertions on the judge. When your opinion does not coincide with his, try and forget your disappointment. There are other shows and other judges, which may mean future triumphs and a sportsmanlike revenge.

In conclusion, I advise all puppies being inoculated before going to a show. They should also be given glycerine of carbolic during the show as a preventative for distemper. Full directions will be found under chapter headed " Distemper."

BREEDING.

In breeding toy dogs of any description, especially where very small specimens are desirable, type is often difficult to maintain without loss of stamina and constitution. I have always held that in order to accomplish satisfactory results one must breed from fairly large brood matrons, though the sire may be as small as you choose, provided he is a vigorous and healthy dog, and of the approved type. The size of toy dogs cannot be regulated by breeding from diminutive specimens. Some of the smallest have been bred from quite large animals, and *vice-versa*. Coarseness in a toy of any kind is to be studiously avoided, though the majority of people err in the other extreme, often breeding from very fine tiny specimens, under the impression that the puppies will also be real midgets. The inadvisability of pursuing this course is evident, for not only do you run a great risk of losing the little mother at the time of whelping, but in all probability she will have but one puppy, which, in the majority of cases, will develop into a large dog, as all her strength and nourishment is given to the " only child." I find that the real midgets belong to big families, as there is always a " runt " in every litter, and great care should be taken to rear this mite, as it will probably be very valuable when matured, and if bred from a large brood matron will be hardier and better fitted to begin his life than the offspring of a diminutive puny bitch.

There are, of course, in some dog families very small bitches with robust constitutions that come from a line of prolific breeders, and will themselves produce tiny pups with plenty of stamina, and yet true to type. Such cases, however, are few and far between, and the novice will be more successful if he follows my advice in this matter, for my experience has been dearly bought, as I lost one of the most beautiful

Served Jan.	Due to Whelp Mar.	Served Feb.	Due to Whelp April	Served Mar.	Due to Whelp May	Served April	Due to Whelp June	Served May	Due to Whelp July	Served June	Due to Whelp Aug.	Served July	Due to Whelp Sept.	Served Aug.	Due to Whelp Oct.	Served Sept.	Due to Whelp Nov.	Served Oct.	Due to Whelp Dec.	Served Nov.	Due to Whelp Jan.	Served Dec.	Due to Whelp Feb.
1	5	1	5	1	3	1	3	1	3	1	3	1	2	1	3	1	3	1	3	1	3	1	2
2	6	2	6	2	4	2	4	2	4	2	4	2	3	2	4	2	4	2	4	2	4	2	3
3	7	3	7	3	5	3	5	3	5	3	5	3	4	3	5	3	5	3	5	3	5	3	4
4	8	4	8	4	6	4	6	4	6	4	6	4	5	4	6	4	6	4	6	4	6	4	5
5	9	5	9	5	7	5	7	5	7	5	7	5	6	5	7	5	7	5	7	5	7	5	6
6	10	6	10	6	8	6	8	6	8	6	8	6	7	6	8	6	8	6	8	6	8	6	7
7	11	7	11	7	9	7	9	7	9	7	9	7	8	7	9	7	9	7	9	7	9	7	8
8	12	8	12	8	10	8	10	8	10	8	10	8	9	8	10	8	10	8	10	8	10	8	9
9	13	9	13	9	11	9	11	9	11	9	11	9	10	9	11	9	11	9	11	9	11	9	10
10	14	10	14	10	12	10	12	10	12	10	12	10	11	10	12	10	12	10	12	10	12	10	11
11	15	11	15	11	13	11	13	11	13	11	13	11	12	11	13	11	13	11	13	11	13	11	12
12	16	12	16	12	14	12	14	12	14	12	14	12	13	12	14	12	14	12	14	12	14	12	13
13	17	13	17	13	15	13	15	13	15	13	15	13	14	13	15	13	15	13	15	13	15	13	14
14	18	14	18	14	16	14	16	14	16	14	16	14	15	14	16	14	16	14	16	14	16	14	15
15	19	15	19	15	17	15	17	15	17	15	17	15	16	15	17	15	17	15	17	15	17	15	16
16	20	16	20	16	18	16	18	16	18	16	18	16	17	16	18	16	18	16	18	16	18	16	17
17	21	17	21	17	19	17	19	17	19	17	19	17	18	17	19	17	19	17	19	17	19	17	18
18	22	18	22	18	20	18	20	18	20	18	20	18	19	18	20	18	20	18	20	18	20	18	19
19	23	19	23	19	21	19	21	19	21	19	21	19	20	19	21	19	21	19	21	19	21	19	20
20	24	20	24	20	22	20	22	20	22	20	22	20	21	20	22	20	22	20	22	20	22	20	21
21	25	21	25	21	23	21	23	21	23	21	23	21	22	21	23	21	23	21	23	21	23	21	22
22	26	22	26	22	24	22	24	22	24	22	24	22	23	22	24	22	24	22	24	22	24	22	23
23	27	23	27	23	25	23	25	23	25	23	25	23	24	23	25	23	25	23	25	23	25	23	24
24	28	24	28	24	26	24	26	24	26	24	26	24	25	24	26	24	26	24	26	24	26	24	25
25	29	25	29	25	27	25	27	25	27	25	27	25	26	25	27	25	27	25	27	25	27	25	26
26	30	26	30	26	28	26	28	26	28	26	28	26	27	26	28	26	28	26	28	26	28	26	27
27	31	27	May 1	27	29	27	29	27	29	27	29	27	28	27	29	27	29	27	29	27	29	27	28
28	April 1	28	May 2	28	30	28	30	28	30	28	30	28	29	28	30	28	30	28	30	28	30	28	Mar. 1
29	2	29	May 3	29	31	29	July 1	29	31	29	31	29	30	29	31	29	Dec. 1	29	31	29	31	29	2
30	3			30	June 1	30	2	30	Aug. 1	30	Sept. 1	30	Oct. 1	30	Nov. 1	30	2	30	Jan. 1	30	Feb. 1	30	3
31	4			31	2			31	2			31	2	31	2			31	2			31	4

85

bitches I ever owned in attempting to breed from too small a specimen.
Let the brood matron be well bred and fairly large, but let her show
quality, as her influence on her progeny may be as strong as that of the
sire.   You cannot expect really good puppies, even if sired by a champion, when the mother is not typical.   The choice of the sire is an all-
important matter, but, as a rule, the best plan to pursue is to select a
dog of fashionable strain, a celebrated prize winner, and successful sire.
You, of course, have no guarantee that the puppies will take after him ;
still, a better price is thereby obtained for them, and if you happen to
hit on the right combination, your future success is assured.   I do not
advocate always breeding to champion dogs, for I have known of many
instances where the great prize-winner has utterly failed as a sire.
The connoisseur will often breed to an unknown and indifferent-
looking little dog, which he knows has the very qualities lacking in his
own strain, but it is not safe for the average breeder to try such
experiments.   Breeding on the line, *i.e.*, from animals whose pedigree
may be traced back to a common ancestor, is the surest way to keep up
the quality of the breed without destroying its distinctive features, and
in this way only can a family likeness be established in the progeny ;
but it must be remembered that it is as easy to perpetuate faults as it is
desirable qualities.   Most doggy families have their weaknesses, therefore care should be observed in the selection of the stud dog, and his
pedigree carefully studied.   Continuous inbreeding is most unwise, as
it invariably produces, in the end, weak and sickly individuals, though
by it any particular characteristic may be accentuated.   In further
reference to the brood matron I may state that unless the bitch is well
matured and at least eight months of age, it is as well to let the first
heat pass before you attempt to breed from her.

A receipt of service should always be given by the person owning
the stud dog, and it is usually the custom for a second service to be
allowed if the bitch fails to prove in whelp.   I should strongly recommend the beginner to procure a kennel register, which can be obtained
for a nominal price from Messrs. Spratt & Co., 25, Fenchurch Street, E.C.
Without such a book it is difficult to keep a detailed account of stud
visits, litters, prizes won, and pedigrees, all of which there is room for
in this useful little volume.   I have found it advisable to dose brood
matrons for worms some time before they are mated, and must emphasise the great importance of food and exercise during the time
of pregnancy.   Gestation lasts sixty-three days, although in
my experience the puppies more often are born on the sixtieth day,
so one must be prepared for them then.   For the last three weeks the

bitch should be fed on light and specially nourishing food, including one meal of finely minced raw beef every day (see page 78). For the last week prior to her confinement she should be given a pinch of flax seed in her food or a teaspoonful of linseed oil once a day, as it is a great assistance to the bitch at time of whelping. Gentle exercise and plenty of fresh air are beneficial, though no long walks or violent running about should be allowed, and great care must be taken that she does not jump on chairs, tear up and down stairs, or in any way strain herself. Such a mishap probably would be followed by a premature birth, and possibly by the death of the matron.

WHELPING.

A week before the date on which the puppies are expected to arrive, the brood bitch should be taken to her new quarters, preferably a quiet room where a comfortable basket or box has been prepared for her. If the proper whelping kennel is not to hand it is best to procure a box with just one very narrow board across the front, so that she can get in and out without hurting herself. An ordinary Tate sugar box will be of sufficient size for toy dogs and can be purchased from your grocer. It should contain a large cushion of sacking filled with clean hay, on which the puppies are to arrive. A fresh bed should also be in readiness, composed of another cushion covered with warm flannel, pillow case, or an old blanket can be used, doubled several times and sewn together, so that the new arrivals cannot crawl in between its folds and get lost, or lain on by their mother. The brood bitch should be encouraged to lie in her new nest and accustom herself to it, so that when the " babies" arrive, she will not drag them all over the house in search of a familiar bed, which is so often the case when this precaution has not been taken. A bowl of fresh water should always be placed where she can conveniently reach it, as bitches are usually feverish and thirsty at this time, and the necessity of providing water for them most important. The bitch's breasts should be thoroughly bathed with Lysol and warm water, or a solution of Kur-mange. just before the puppies are due, and also occasionally whilst she is nursing them. This is done to destroy worm larva, which otherwise may be sucked in by the puppies and cause endless trouble.

When the eventful day arrives, if the weather is chilly, a fire should be lighted and the room kept at an even temperature. A hot-water bottle should be provided in a cosy basket lined with flannel, into which Master Puppy will contentedly snuggle and take a nap, while his small brothers and sisters are being brought into the world. It is much wiser to remove each puppy to this basket after the mother has completed his toilet, and when it becomes apparent that another one is shortly to be born. If they are all left in the nest, they run great risks of being crushed, or of being pushed into a cold corner by the mother, while she is giving her attention to the latest arrival.

When all the little ones have safely arrived, the entire family may be transferred to the soft flannel bed which should previously have been warmed by the fire. If the bitch appears to have great difficulty in whelping, and if no puppies appear after she has been in labour for some hours, I should strongly advise the novice to call in a competent veterinary surgeon, as some slight help may save valuable puppies if quickly and skilfully given, and I do not consider that any but experienced people should attempt to interfere with a bitch in trouble at this time. In normal cases the puppies are born in a bag of thin elastic membrane, which the mother should strip open with her teeth at once, and lick the puppy dry. The umbilical cord which attaches the puppy's abdomen to the placenta or afterbirth (a soft, blackish looking substance) is then bitten through and the placenta swallowed. In nine cases out of ten the mother's natural instinct leads her to do all that is necessary, so it is best not to interfere with her at all unless she is either too weak or too indifferent to remove the membrane herself. In this event the puppy must be released and given air, or it will suffocate very quickly if allowed to remain for more than a couple of minutes in its little bag. The umbilical cord should never be cut until the afterbirth has all come away, otherwise the latter will most likely slip back into the womb and cause blood poisoning ; if, however, it becomes absolutely necessary to free the puppy, the afterbirth must be very gently extracted and then the umbilical cord should be tied with strong white embroidery silk about three-quarters of an inch from the abdomen and cut with blunt scissors just below where it is tied. The bit that remains will very soon dry up and drop off. The removing of the afterbirth is a very ticklish business for any but experienced breeders to attempt, and it should never be undertaken by the novice except as a last resource. After her family has all arrived the little mother should be given a good drink of warm milk and then left undisturbed with her babies for some hours, when she should be taken out for five minutes' exercise. The following day she may be kept away for twenty minutes, gradually increasing the time, for as the puppies gain in strength and size they become a great strain on her, and if she is not kept away from them a sufficient time the consequence will probably be fever and suckling fits.

These fits are very common at such times to highly bred animals of a nervous temperament, but can easily be avoided if the bitch is carefully watched and removed at the first suspicion to some quiet spot and away from her puppies for some hours, and given a small dose of bromide (see " Fits "). The symptoms are feverishness, excessive panting, a curious twitching of the limbs and general uneasiness. If the patient is taken in hand before she gets worse, the cure will be quickly accomplished, but if neglected she will develop terrible convulsions. In severe cases the suppression of milk is complete, and it will be necessary to feed the pups by hand. In fact, it is advisable to feed them in any case, even if the mother has only to be kept away for a few hours, and if she is not allowed to nurse them till she has fully recovered so much the better. It is, of course, understood that while the bitch is in retirement the puppies must be kept snug and warm, and the hot water bottle used (rolled in flannel at the bottom of the nest) if the weather is at all chilly. This is the best substitute for a Roger's Puppy Breeder which many breeders are not lucky enough to possess.

Another cause of trouble which must be carefully guarded against, and which is very common, is the congealing of the milk in some of the little mother's breasts, due to the puppies not suckling from them. It will be usually noticed the day after whelping that these breasts have become hard and inflamed, and it will be necessary to gently draw off the milk with one's fingers and to bathe the affected parts in warm water. This will soon restore the breasts to their normal state, and if the puppies can be induced to suckle them all will be well. Neglected, serious results may ensue, and an abscess form which causes great pain, and will have to be poulticed, or perhaps lanced. The proper food to give will be found under " Feeding."

CATS AS FOSTER MOTHERS.

Few people know the value of cats as foster mothers and I should probably have never known myself but for the following experience which I am going to relate. Some years ago I had two litters of puppies (five in each lot) born the same day. There were four big strong puppies in each litter and one atom in each. It was evident from the beginning that the small ones would starve if left with the mothers, because directly they attempted to take any nourishment they were pushed to one side by the bigger puppies. I tried spoon and bottle feeding for a time, but it was an endless task, as the puppies had to be fed every two hours, night and day, and kept on a hot water bottle which also required constant replenishing. Unfortunately I had no Rogers Puppy Brooder at that time. I was getting very tired and worried, when I suddenly remembered that my big Persian cat had some kittens born a couple of days before, and I wondered if she would make a capable foster mother for my tiny puppies. To my great delight she welcomed the puppies with open arms, licked them all over, and coddled them up to her in the most motherly fashion, and in less time than it takes to write it the two imps were hard at work, and from their grunts of satisfaction I imagined that they were having a very good breakfast. To make a long story short, "Kittens" (this is the cat's name) reared my two tiny Pekes, and she brought them up in the most exemplary manner. They were as plump as partridges when weaned, and to this day, although both are grown dogs, they love their foster mother, and she loves them, and it is very sweet to see them all playing about together. I was so delighted with my foster mother that ever since I have kept two or three Persian cats for this purpose, and many a "sleeve" puppy have they reared for me which would otherwise have had no chance at all if left in the nest with his larger brothers and sisters. A cat's body is warmer than a dog's, and besides, she does not leave the puppies as much as a dog would do, and she never "squashes " one, therefore she is an ideal foster mother for a small or delicate puppy.

At least one kitten should be left with the mother for a couple of days or until she has quite adopted her " foster children," when it may be taken away and destroyed. A good cat will rear from 3 to 4 puppies at a time if required.

REARING.

Puppies should remain with their mother till they are six or seven weeks old, but from the time they are a month old they should receive additional nourishment, as prescribed under " Feeding." If the mother dies or is for some other reason unable to nurse her family, it will be necessary either to secure a foster-mother or to feed them by hand. This is by no means an easy task, and not always successful if the babies are very young, as much handling is injurious. Then, too, it is difficult to substitute anything as nice and warm as the mother's body against which the poor little orphans can nestle, though I have found my old standby, the hot-water bottle, covered with some soft woolly material in a flannel-lined basket, the best substitute, unless the luxury of a Roger's Brooder is available.

At first, the food should be malted milk, blood warm, and the quantity about two teaspoonsful every two hours *night and day*, which interval should be gradually increased as the pups gain in size and strength. An ordinary baby's bottle, which is often used successfully with the larger breeds, is too big for " toys," so in order to get a very small nipple, I have found it advisable to use the rubber top off an eye dropper, and to make a hole in it by means of a red-hot hat pin. Other plans are to fill an ordinary dropper with milk, insert it into the puppy's mouth, and press gently, or to feed from an egg-spoon.

Happiness and health go hand in hand, so the happier you make your puppies the healthier they will be, and the better able to withstand the numerous complaints of puppyhood to which they are heir. It is not wise to dose young puppies for worms (see chapter on " Worms.") instead, they should be given good, nourishing food, which in time ought to tone up their systems, and then when strong enough the medicine may be administered, but care must be taken not to risk this too soon, for many valuable pups have been lost through undue haste in the matter.

I examine my puppies thoroughly every few days, so that a cold or slight skin eruption may be detected and treated in time, thus checking what might have developed into a serious illness. Let them have a warm and cosy bed to lie in when first taken from their mother, and cover them up at night if the weather is at all chilly. Personally, I use a combination whelping and breeding kennel (my own design), for puppies from the time they are born until they are able to run about well. The bitch sleeps in it before the puppies are born, whelps in it, and rears her pups in it as long as they remain in the nest. It is 4ft. by 1½ft. by 2ft. with wooden sides and back, a lid which lifts up and a wire front made on a stout wooden frame to lift in and out. There is a nice roomy sleeping compartment boarded off inside, and a zinc lined drawer on which newspaper is laid. For some time past I have given up the use of sawdust in my kennel. It gets into the puppies' eyes and coats, also over their cushions, and generally makes a mess of everything. Newspaper is infinitely cleaner, and I think that anyone who has once used it for their dogs will never go back to sawdust. From the time my puppies are able to walk I teach them to go to the newspaper to attend to their small wants. All dogs are naturally clean and a little patience will soon teach them house manners. After a few days the door of the kennel may be left open and the puppies allowed to run about in a small enclosure made outside, and they will always be found to return to their newspaper lavatory. Later on, when given the freedom of the room, they will know what to do. They are always shut inside the kennel at night, and when three months old, if the weather permits, are taken outdoors and given a short run early in the morning, and at regular intervals during the day. In this way they will learn cleanliness, and no whippings or other methods will be necessary, but it must be borne in mind that the earlier you take the puppies in hand the easier it will be to train them.

Puppies naturally take lots of exercise, but it is unwise to allow them to play too hard or to go for long walks till they have attained maturity, as running exercise has a tendency to make the legs long and enlarge the joints, both most undesirable features in a toy dog.

As to the proper food for young puppies see chapter on " Feeding."

THE VALUE OF NURSING.

The general health of a pet dog should be carefully attended to, as it is easier to prevent disease than to cure it. If the eyes are inflamed, and the nose hot and dry, or the gums pale, it is a sure indication that something is wrong and needs putting right. Change of air and diet will sometimes recruit a dog without the aid of medicine ; however, in the case of serious illness, good nursing is half the battle, and to be " always ready for the enemy " is a golden rule which should never be forgotten. The sick room should be kept at an even temperature, well ventilated (though without draughts), a comfortable bed supplied, extreme cleanliness observed, and only the best of food provided, which should be made very tempting.

A very sick dog needs nourishment at intervals during the entire twenty-four hours, so to be in constant attendance night and day is a chief desideratum. If possible, medicines should be administered by the patient's mistress, or someone known to him, as a pet dog frequently becomes greatly upset when left entirely to the care of strangers, so that a nervous animal may receive many setbacks in this way. Food, too, will always be more welcome from a familiar hand, for the small canines are more sensitive than many people realise, and a little sympathy or coddling will often do much towards ensuring a cure.

A sick dog should be treated with as much care as if he were a sick child, and his food prepared in exactly the same careful manner. Practically any of the excellent preparations used for human invalids will do equally well for the little sick canine. The dietary recommended by me under heading of " Feeding," which has been so successfully used in my own kennels, will undoubtedly prove beneficial to others. In serious illness the patient's strength must be kept up above all things, and should he absolutely refuse to eat, nourishment must be given to him in small quantities, and at short intervals. To do this successfully one must proceed very gently, as on no account must the dog be allowed to get excited in his weakened condition. In administering liquid nourishment or medicine, the animal's head should be slightly raised, and his lower lip drawn out from the teeth so as to form a pouch into which the liquor can be poured by means of a spoon. If he does not swallow it immediately, gently rubbing the windpipe will have the desired effect. An experienced nurse can usually manage this alone, and by exceeding gentleness and care will succeed in feeding the dog without tiring him or exciting him in the slightest.

Solid food is advisable, even in infinitesimal quantities, as an exhausted stomach will frequently rebel against the continued use of liquid nourishment. A plan which seldom fails to tempt the most fastidious individuals is the old trick of pretending to eat the food yourself, then offering it to the dog. Many and many a time have I seen a goodly meal made in this way, and many a sweet little life has been saved by it I know.

Liquid medicines are comparatively easy of administration, but it is not so with pills, which should be given as follows :—Raise the head slightly, and drop the pill well back into the mouth, then with your finger push it down his throat, close the mouth, rub the throat gently, and the dog will swallow it. A competent nurse must understand how to take her patient's temperature, and in serious illness it is most important to keep a chart just like the one used by trained nurses, and to have the same carefully made out for the vet's inspection, as well as for your now use. It can be kept on an ordinary large pad, on which spaces have been ruled off, for date and time, food, medicine, temperature, remarks (the latter including condition of the bowels, etc., etc.), and if spaces are required for pulse, respirations, or anything else, they can of course be added. By this means you will be enabled to see at a glance the amount of nourishment the dog is getting, and there is never any danger of making a mistake in his medicine when each dose is entered, and the hour at which it was given.

The pulse can easily be felt by placing your finger on the large artery at the inside of the upper portion of the hind-leg. The normal state of a toy dog's pulse is about eighty beats to a minute, while in illness it runs up to one hundred and fifty, though only in very serious cases. The pulsations may be counted by the second-hand of a watch, and after a little practice you will know immediately whether the pulse is slow or fast, or if it is strong. In taking a dog's temperature a very small clinical thermometer (which should always be kept in the house) is dipped with the mercury end foremost into vaseline, and inserted very gently into the rectum, kept there from one to three minutes, removed, and the number of degrees registered carefully noted. The temperature of a healthy dog when obtained in this way is one hundred and one while during illness it frequently runs up to one hundred and four, and even reaches one hundred and six degrees, though such cases usually prove fatal.

Where any number of toy dogs are kept, it is a very good plan, if possible, to set aside one room at the top of the house as a permanent hospital, whence they can be immediately removed from their companions the moment disease is apparent. Medicines can always be kept there, and everything will be in readiness to receive the patient, and the house will not be turned upside down, as is often the case when illness suddenly arises. The hospital should have a bright and cheery aspect, and, if possible, a fireplace, as I do not like the heat of a stove, and it is often necessary to keep a kettle boiling in the room. Small kennels, with wire doors, raised about a foot from the floor, are advisable, and can be made most comfortable with a soft cushion for the dog to lie on. Baskets are too draughty, and an armchair, which some people prefer, while undoubtedly a cosy nest, is usually most difficult to disinfect, and there is always a chance of the dog's falling out of it, and so injuring himself.

Apropos of disinfectants, I may mention here that Sanitas, Jey's Izal and Formalin are excellent for general use, but I prefer Lysol for internal use, or for bathing wounds. For washing kennels, floors, etc., after a contagious disease, use one-half a pint of crude carbolic acid to every large pail of water, but it may be well to point out the danger of such powerful poisons unless the greatest care is taken when using them. Leicester's formalin candles should be burned in the hospital immediately after the patient has been removed, and feeding utensils thoroughly sterilized, but the flannel jackets used for diseases of the chest and distemper must be burned, as well as all the cushions and anything else likely to harbour germs. In regard to these little jackets it is a good idea to have several on hand, ready for emergency ; directions for making will be found under " Distemper." I will again call attention to the urgent necessity for good and capable nursing in all cases of canine illness, and I feel that I cannot be too emphatic on this point. Kindness, tact, and strategy, coupled with a certain amount of experience and fondness for animals are essential to this end, and the woman who combines these qualities should be able to manage her own kennel with the greatest success.

DOCTORING.

Before entering into the many troubles which beset our canine friends, it may be well to point out here that it is impossible to lay down any hard and fast rules in regard to doctoring as the same medicines will not suit every individual. Dogs differ broadly in temperament and constitution, and for that reason when giving medicine its effects upon each dog should be carefully noted. The owner must use her own judgment as to whether the dose is too strong or too weak, or whether it is doing good or the reverse. In my advice as to treatment of sick animals throughout this little book, I am prescribing for small dogs, and have selected Pekingese as a type. All of the medicines mentioned I have used while success in my own kennels, while the various foods have all been tried by me and found most valuable. The following is merely intended to help the amateur to properly diagnose an attack of illness, and to know which medicine to use in mild cases, or when medical aid is unobtainable ; but I must frankly say that where poisoning or serious illness is suspected, it would be exceedingly unwise to trust entirely to her own judgment. Rather let her send for a payable vet., and see that his instructions are carried out to the letter.

DISTEMPER.

This is one of the most fatal maladies which attack dogs, and probably claims more victims than any other disease. It is known in three forms, *i.e.*, of the head, lungs, and bowels. Young puppies are most susceptive to its ravages, and those which are often shown seldom escape, for distemper is both contagious and infectious. It is not of spontaneous origin, as many people believe, but is due to a specific virus.

Dogs suffering from this disease must be strictly quarantined, and those returning from shows should on no account be allowed near young puppies. It is commonly believed that one attack gives immunity from a subsequent one, yet such is not always the case. One of my own Yorkshires had a bad case of distemper when he was a puppy, and again at eight years of age, though as a rule if your dog has been through distemper he is pretty safe. Careful nursing is half the battle in conquering this fatal trouble, and to be always ready for the enemy is of equal importance, for there is no disease which prostrates the system so quickly, and when once it gains headway a cure cannot always be ensured even by the most skilful.   It should be taken in hand at the first warning, and very tempting food given to the little invalid to keep up his strength.

Distemper usually runs from three to six weeks, its first symptoms being rise of temperature, general debility, loss of appetite, feverishness, followed by a husky cough, or severe sneezing, running from the eyes and nose, and offensive breath.   My first plan, after having taken the dog's temperature, and found it above normal, is to isolate him at once. If possible it is best to use a bright cheerful room at the top of the house, which must be kept at an even temperature and well ventilated, while draughts must be rigorously avoided.   A kettle should be kept

A Flannel Coat, covering the chest, useful in cases of distemper and in all lung trouble.

boiling on the fire, and about a dessertspoonful of eucalyptus oil added to the water.   This greatly assists the patient's breathing, and also helps to disinfect the air.   The dog should be sewn into a flannel jacket (which, if the lungs are affected, must be lined with Thermogene wool).   (See illustration).   It can easily be made to fit, allowing two holes for his little front feet and one for the neck as well ;   then it should be securely sewed up the back.   It need not cover more than one-half of his body, the principal object of the jacket being to protect the chest and lungs.   For lung complications, see " Pneumonia." This done, I begin giving my old standby, glycerine of carbolic, the prescription for which I have to thank the celebrated English animal painter and well-known fancier, Miss Fairman, who gave it to me some years ago. The proportions are : One part of carbolic to ten of glycerine. When this is given very little medicine will be necessary, as it thoroughly disinfects the dog's whole system, and prevents his getting the disease in its worst forms. I have dosed hundreds of dogs in this way with simply phenomenal success, and I consider it by far the most valuable discovery in this line. It is also a capital preventative of distemper, and should be given to all dogs in a kennel infected with this disease and also to those sent to shows. I have done my share of showing during the past years, and in no single case have I brought back distemper, and I believe that it was wholly due to the fact that my dogs were given eight drops of glycerine of carbolic twice a day while they were on exhibition, and that they were all inoculated with Professor Woodroff Hill's wonderful threads previous to being shown.

In severe cases of distemper the carbolic mixture may be administered every four hours, but usually three times a day will be sufficient, the quantities varying from three drops for a six-weeks-old puppy to twenty drops for a twelve-pound dog, and should be given in a teaspoonful of water. I must also mention another excellent preparation known as The Doctor's Distemper Mixture. It is good for any sort of cold, and is largely used by many well-known exhibitors as a preventative for distemper. The temperature of a sick dog should be taken twice daily, and if he has a fever it must be reduced. (See " Fever.") The bowels must be carefully regulated also. In case of constipation, give a gentle laxative, but for diarrhoea (most common at this time) I have found a small teaspoonful of tincture of rhubarb mixed with a little warm water and given three times a day of great benefit, or a five-grain salol tablet night and morning for a grown dog, and half the quantity for a puppy. Carefully prepared arrowroot, to which a few drops of brandy have been added, is often effective, and for young puppies the safest thing to use. (See Diarrhoea).

Vomiting frequently causes much trouble, and unless checked will often prove fatal. Try my pet prescription of Bi-carbonate of soda or Bismuth (see Gastritis) and if this fails to relieve give twenty drops of five-per-cent. solution of cocain, to be repeated in twenty minutes. It must be remembered that when the vomiting has ceased, great care must be taken not to overload the stomach, and the diet must be specially digestible. Liquid beef peptonoids I prefer to anything else ; in fact, I advise giving it all through a case of distemper. Valuable at all times, it is especially so when the stomach is very weak, and will be retained when all else fails. The proper method of feeding will be found under its own heading, but it is well to emphasise here the great

H

necessity of giving plenty of nourishment to dogs suffering from distemper, and that quality is the important thing. When the convalescent stage is reached, the following Tonic Pills will be found useful : Quinine nine grains, sulphur of iron thirteen grains, extract of gentian eighteen grains, powdered sugar thirteen grains ; make into a dozen pills and give one night and morning.

FITS.

Fits arise from various causes, and are generally classed as epileptic, apoplectic, distemper, teething, those due to worms, and suckling fits. It is not my intention to go fully into this matter, but merely to mention a few simple remedies which I have found most effective. Beginning with *suckling fits*, these are caused by exhaustion consequent on the inability of the brood-bitch to suckle so many puppies, or by her having been left in too constant attendance on them. (See "Breeding"). A bitch in this condition shows extreme exhaustion, she lies or falls down, breathing heavily, her limbs twitching, with nose hot and dry. Remove her instantly from her puppies (which should be kept warm in a Rogers Puppy Brooder) and fed on Horlick's Malted Milk until she is sufficiently recovered to return to them). In all cases, a cold wet cloth, or ice in an oil-skin bag, must be kept on her head until the fever is reduced, and twitching ceases, and she should be given from 3 to 5 grains of bromide of potassium diluted in a teaspoonful of water. It may be repeated every two hours if the patient is still suffering, then twice daily till she is herself again.

The bitch must, of course, be kept very quiet, and should be given light nourishment, such as rice and milk, paunch, the white of eggs, chicken or rabbit, but no red meat, for a day or so till she has fully regained her strength, or if she is very weak give in addition a dessert-spoonful of liquid beef peptonoids three times a day. When she is returned to her little ones she must be carefully watched and not left with them too long at a time, or another attack will certainly follow. Aperient medicines should always be administered as soon as possible, liquid paraffin for preference and the bowels well looked to until the attack has passed. Where pain is present codine given in quarter-grain doses one hour apart (only two doses) will quiet the little patient and lessen the pain to a wonderful degree. Bromide of potassium can be used for any sort of fit arising from excitement, and for apoplexy in old dogs it will be found a capital cure. I always have some ready for use at dog shows, where puppies are frequently taken with convulsions due to over-excitement. There is yet another remedy for bitches suffering from suckling fits which is a drastic one, and should only be used when all others fail. It is almost too heroic a treatment for toy dogs, though an excellent one for larger breeds. Prepare a tub of warm water (98 Fahrenheit), and place the patient in it so that she is completely covered with water up to the neck. She should be kept in this bath from ten to twenty minutes, until the twitching subsides, hot water being occasionally added to keep the bath at an even temperature. Then dry quickly with a rough towel, roll in a blanket, and keep her in some dark or very quiet spot where she will probably fall asleep, and should be left undisturbed till she awakens. For fits caused by distemper, give bromide as previously mentioned. In slight cases of fits in puppies, a little opening medicine will often be all that is needed, unless the trouble is caused by worms, when vermifuges should be administered. It is a mistake to pour cold water all over a dog in a fit, the head only should be wet, and in all cases the patient kept very quiet.

INDIGESTION.

Indigestion is a disorder that is often the cause of much trouble to growing puppies when their cases have not been properly diagnosed. Many people mistake the symptoms for those of worms, and dose their dogs accordingly, with the result that the vermifuges only aggravate the trouble, and the dog gets rapidly worse. It is usually brought on by want of exercise, improper food, or irregularity of meals. The first move is to ascertain the cause of the trouble, and then to proceed with the remedies prescribed as thoroughly as possible, always remembering that proper and regular meals, and plenty of fresh air, with walking exercise, will materially assist, and in many cases accomplish a complete cure. The usual symptoms are constipation, accompanied by flatulency, a depraved and fitful appetite, and occasionally vomiting. The dog seems feverish and ill at ease, and in most cases is exceedingly peevish. A purgative is advisable to relieve the bowels, or, if necessary, an enema. For flatulency, three grains of carbonate of bismuth may be given dry, upon the tongue three times a day. The food must be light and easy of digestion, and lime-water should be added to the drinking water or milk. Pepsin is also most essential, and can be given in the food, pepsine tabloids being the most reliable as well as the most convenient form of giving it. Peptonized milk, beef, or chicken, however, is probably better in chronic or obstinate cases. The peptonizing powders can be obtained at any chemist's, and contain full directions for use.

Strict attention must be paid to the diet, for unless this detail is carefully attended to you cannot expect success. The only safe plan is to personally superintend both the feeding and preparation of the food, or, better still, to do it yourself. Few servants will take sufficient trouble, and still fewer are capable of using the proper judgment in an important matter of this kind.

CONSTIPATION.

Constipation is one of the ills most prevalent among highly-fed pet dogs, which if neglected assumes a chronic form, usually culminating in some obstinate skin trouble. Dogs that are much confined are also liable to this disorder, or it may be coexistent with some other disease. In any event, the first thing to be done is to remove the primary cause, which may be accomplished by various means. A soap and warm water enema will usually have the desired effect, or a small piece of softish common soap about an inch long and the thickness of a pencil, inserted in the rectum and kept there for some minutes, seldom fails to relieve. It is a great mistake to give strong purgatives for constipation, but a dessert-spoonful of liquid paraffin or pure olive oil with ten drops of buckthorne is advisable, and should be repeated daily till the bowels have assumed their normal condition. Change of diet is likewise essential, and daily exercise in the open air. As a sluggish liver has a great deal to do with this complaint, one-fourth-grain doses of calomel, twice a day for two days, in addition to the other remedies, is always advisable ; or else half a cascara pill given twice daily. In case of pain give two doses of one-fourth of a grain of codine one hour apart. This drug is invaluable in all cases of intestinal pain, and is perfectly safe to give in above quantities. The menu should be varied, consisting of somewhat sloppy mixtures, and a liberal proportion of well-cooked vegetables. Finely chopped boiled calves' liver at least every third day will be beneficial.

I must remark, however, that constipation is, in nine cases out of ten, the result of carelessness, in not paying proper attention to the all-important factors of food and exercise. If grown dogs are properly fed and are not confined too closely, there is no reason why they should be troubled with this complaint. With puppies, of course, it is different, for with them it may arise from worms or in consequence of a change in the quality of their mother's milk. In old dogs, it is sometimes brought on by other complications, but with young and healthy animals carelessness and neglect are alone responsible.

DIARRHOEA.

Diarrhoea is a common complaint with dogs, particularly during puppyhood, and as there are many remedies varying with the violence of the disease, I must leave a large margin to the discretion of my readers as to which of the following to use.

For small puppies, a dose of slightly warmed olive oil (from one to two teaspoonfuls) should be given at the commencement of an attack, three to five drops of laudanum being added if there seems to be much pain attending the trouble. When the effects of the oil has worked off, give three grains of bismuth on the tongue three times daily.

A rather stronger remedy, which I have found very effectual, is burnt brandy, prepared by setting fire to a small quantity of brandy in a dessert-spoon, till the alcohol is burned away. Dose, from three to thirty drops. Arrowroot mixed with a little milk has a binding effect, and is a safe though mild remedy.

For adults one dessert-spoonful of liquid paraffin (in order to remove the irritating cause) should be given at once, followed in about four hours by five grains of carbonate of bismuth on the tongue three times a day, but for more obstinate cases a dose of tamialum (five grains three times a day) is often successful.

Another strong astringent is an injection of about a table-spoonful of thin starch to which five drops of laudanum have been added. This is particularly soothing to the bowels, and should be sufficient to check the severest form of this troublesome complaint. It should not be resorted to, however, until the oil and bismuth has had a fair trial.

In all cases great attention must be paid to the subsequent dieting of the patient to prevent a recurrence of the trouble. Light and easily digested food is essential, boiled milk slightly thickened with arrowroot, beef tea, or corn flour mixed with gelatine, may be given with good results. Scraped raw beef, and malted milk tablets, also arrowroot biscuits should always be given, and I have known a hard-boiled egg to act like magic when all other foods had failed. No one food will suit all dogs in this tiresome complaint, so one after the other must be tried till you hit upon the right one. A small quantity of lime-water must be mixed with the drinking water, and in severe cases barley water used exclusively. If the patient is greatly reduced in strength, a new-laid egg beaten up with a little port wine, or brandy, is excellent, and liquid beef peptonoids given in quantities of a dessert-spoonful twice daily will be found an excellent tonic. Should dysentery supervene, my advice is to seek veterinary aid at once, for this disease is not alone most dangerous in itself, but is frequently the prelude of inflammation of the bowels and peritonitis.

COLIC.

This trouble is especially prevalent among puppies, though it attacks older animals as well, and unless speedily checked may develop into that exceedingly dangerous malady, inflammation of the bowels. The amateur can readily distinguish between these two, as fever and general disorganisation are forerunners of the latter, which comes on gradually, while the colic attacks suddenly. The animal, when apparently in perfect health, is seized with spasm, and cries out, and as the paroxysms of pain increase he draws himself together, rolls over and over, and shows every indication of intense agony. His eyes, too, assume an expression of suffering, and the poor little mouth is drawn and pinched. In prescribing for young puppies I prefer the use of laudanum, as the action of this drug is exceedingly rapid (dose, from three to six drops, according to size), as it affords almost instantaneous relief from excruciating pain, which is bound to seriously weaken a young or delicate puppy. If the attack is very acute, a little brandy may be added, but in mild cases ten drops of Woodward's Gripe Water (as given to children) or else one-half teaspoonful of Pitcher's Castoria will often have the desired effect, especially if flatulency is present. The stomach should be gently massaged, hot flannels applied, and liquid paraffin given. A hot-water bottle in a cosy flannel-lined basket makes a nice warm nest, where the poor litle sufferer can lie when the attack has subsided.

Grown dogs may be treated in pretty much the same way, but the medicines prescribed should be of a stronger nature. The laudanum already mentioned will do for them in doses varying from six to ten drops, while if the pain is very great give the following : Tincture of opium, 5 drops ; chloral, 3 grains. Personally, I have seldom used anything but laudanum and Castoria, and consider that both should be included in the dog's medicine chest. For a few days after the attack has passed away, keep up a laxative diet, and see that the dog has specially comfortable quarters to sleep in, and that his exercise is of the mildest nature.

POISON.

The symptoms which should lead one to suspect poisoning may be distinguished generally from those of disease by the suddenness of the attack and the chance of the dog having come in contact with any poisonous substance. Speaking generally, the first thing to do when poisoning is suspected is to send swiftly for medical aid, and in the meantime to administer an emetic and to continue it till vomiting is fully established. Salt and water is commonly used, or a weak solution of mustard and water, giving about half a cupful to begin with. When the emetic has had the desired effect, give white of egg, and wait the arrival of the doctor.

In the event of his services not being available, the following information is given : The most common form of poisoning is by strychnine, which shows itself in the following way. The dog affected is seized with convulsions, accompanied by champing of the jaws and intermittent twitching of the limbs. He frequently utters loud cries, falls on his side, and when quite exhausted, his limbs become rigid. The antidote for this poison is syrup of chloral, of which a teaspoonful in water should be given as soon as the dog has been made sick.

The symptoms of poisoning by arsenic, which is of rarer occurrence than the last, are restlessness, intense thirst, violent inflammation of the stomach, frequent vomiting and reaching, and diarrhoea. The dog's breath is laboured and painful, the pulse becomes feeble and quick, death generally following in a few hours. Treatment : Give the emetic and white of egg as above (flour and water will take the place of white of egg if the latter is not procurable). Antidote : Ten drops of tincture of iron in a teaspoonful of water.

EAR CANKER.

There are two kinds of canker, internal and external. They are easy to detect, and an ounce of prevention is worth a pound of cure. The former is caused by inflammation of the membrane lining the passage to the ear ; ulceration follows, and if not treated at once, a blackish fluid is discharged, which eventually fills up the ear and throws off a most offensive odour. The itching caused by this eruption is so intense that a dog afflicted in this way will hold his head on one side, giving it violent shakes, and constantly scratch his ear. Canker arises from many causes, but the most common is neglect.

The ear is a very sensitive part of a dog's anatomy, and a wise owner will regularly examine them and see that they are properly cleaned at least once a week. This is a very simple operation, and can be accomplished by using a small swab of cotton on the end of a match. In treating mild cases of internal caker I cannot do better that recommend the use of Shirley's Canker Lotion. Repeat every day till a cure is effected. In more obstinate cases it is often necessary to remove any accumulation of dirt or wax. To do this pour into the ear a few drops of warm olive oil, and when the wax becomes soft pick it out by means of the cotton swab previously mentioned. Then dry carefully with medicated cotton wool, and use Shirley's Canker Lotion as before.

External canker is a sort of mangy affection of the ear flap. It is well to give the patient an aperient, then to carefully bathe the inflamed parts with rather a strong solution of Kur-mange and warm water, and after a thorough drying to apply the following ointment (" My own prescription ") :   Powdered Magnesia, 4 tablespoonfuls ;   powdered sulphur, 2 teaspoonfuls ;   powdered Starch, 2 teaspoonfuls ;   powdered Boracic Acid, 2 teaspoonfuls ;   add   sufficient   lime-water to make the consistency of thick cream. It is wonderfully cooling, and will cure in a remarkably short time the worst cases of any inflammation of the skin. Resinol, also Beta Naptha ointment are also very good, and it is sometimes necessary to try several remedies before the right one is found, as the same dressing will not cure every case.

MANGE.

There are two kinds of mange, follicular and sarcoptic, the latter showing itself by the presence of pimples, which after a time break and discharge, and the skin becomes harsh and dry, while the former makes its appearance in small red spots, and if not checked the whole body becomes affected. This kind of mange is especially obstinate to cure, and will frequently break out again. The first symptoms usually appear in scurfy spots about the joints of the legs, over the eyes, and on the ears, and in the hair falling off in patches. If taken in hand immediately a cure is usually no difficult matter, but neglect the dog and in a short time he will be in a pitiable condition, and sometimes " past praying for."   I am going to mention three different remedies for this very unpleasant disease for there are so many kinds of skin trouble that the same prescription will not suit all cases and it may be necessary to try them all before the right one is found. My advice is, first of all, have the dog washed in a preparation known as Kurmange, of which I cannot speak too highly, it is good for any kind of parasitic skin trouble, and is very easily applied. The dog should be washed in it twice a week and dried without rinsing. The second is a very old mange dressing which many people still swear by. but I personally do not like it, as the dog has to be kept soaked in it and closely confined for days at a time, and the smell is very unpleasant. The treatment is a good warm bath, using plenty of soap, then after he has been thoroughly dried, saturate him with the following mixture :—Mange dressing : Powdered sulphur, 2lbs. ; carbonate of soda, 2oz. ; oil of tar, 2oz. ; crude oil, 3 pints ; cotton seed oil, 5 pints. Apply daily for four days, then wash the dog, and saturate him again. It will take from three to six weeks to effect a complete cure. If the irritation is confined to the joints alone, dab on the dressing, as in such cases it will not be necessary to put the whole dog " in pickle." Mange in any phase is fearfully contagious, but when the subject is covered with dressing, there is little or no danger of his transmitting it. The third remedy is the strongest of all. It is merely a solution of sulphurated potash and I have never known it to fail if properly applied, but where most amateurs err is in the way they apply the above prescriptions. It must be thoroughly done, and continued until the cure is complete, otherwise the dog will only break out again, and much valuable time will have been lost.

Dissolve 4 oz. of sulphurated potash in 2 gallons of warm water and stand the dog in it up to his neck for five minutes, then dry without rinsing. Repeat this operation to begin with every 4 days, then once a week until he is perfectly well.

I might mention that in bad cases of skin trouble the dog must be clipped from head to tail. You can cure him in half the time if this is done, and the coat will come in much thicker and better than if left on the dog to fall out by degrees as it will surely do. Mange is by no means difficult to cure ; it simply requires patience and strict attention to all details with regard to the above treatment. When the dog is himself again, everything that he has used must be well disinfected or else destroyed or he will become re-infected again. Such things as rugs, carpets, cushions, kennels, etc., being frightfully contagious.

In mange, as in all skin diseases, the blood is more or less affected, and the patient will be all the better for a course of blood tonic (see " Eczema ") administered twice daily in a little water after meals. It is also well to remember that the bowels must be kept regular, and very little cooked meat allowed.

ECZEMA.

Eczema is a very troublesome complaint. It is non-contagious, and usually arises from overfeeding, too much meat, lack of exercise, and worms. Brood matrons suffer from a kind of eczema which appears after the puppies are weaned ; this, however, is of no great significance, and can be readily cured. In all cases, I should recommend giving a brisk purgative followed by a warm bath, and when the patient is perfectly dry cover him with : Olive oil, one pint ; oil of tar, two ounces ; and sulphur, quarter pound. Apply as for mange dressing.

Another sort of eczema is that which appears like beads of perspiration inside the ear flap and between the toes. This is very contagious, but is soon cured by a few application of Kur-Mange or Resinol or Beta-Naptha ointment applied after the affected parts have been well dried with medicated cotton wool.

As it is important to produce a healthier condition of the blood, the following mixture will be of great help ; dose, a dessert-spoonful night and morning after food. Blood Tonic : Donovan's solution, 1 dr. ; Epsom salts, 1 oz. ; tincture of ginger, 2 drs. ; water, 6 ozs. I am also a great believer in Benbows, and consider it worth its weight in gold as a blood tonic and conditioner.

PLEURISY.

A very painful and exceedingly weakening malady, producing much the same symptoms as pneumonia, and consequently should be treated in the same way. In all cases where the lungs are affected it is wiser to call in a Vet., as a step in the wrong direction may mean the loss of a valuable dog. This trouble is particularly quick in its development, and like pneumonia much depends upon relieving the congestion of the lungs in its early stages. I am opposed to the use of counter-irritants, such as mustard or turpentine poultices for the chest, as such only increase the animal's suffering. Something soothing, such as camphorated oil, or a nice warm flaxseed poultice to draw out the pain, are far more beneficial. The latter should only be applied by a qualified nurse because it will do more harm than good if not properly done, or if the dog is allowed to take chill afterwards. Iodex (see " Influenza ") or Antiphrogistine are also very helpful in bad cases, and are the safer poultices for the amateur to use. The dog's hair must be shaved off in the region of the lungs and a thick layer of the Antiphrogistine pasted on as warm as possible and covered quickly with gamgee wool held in place by means of a flannel jacket. As dogs are very thirsty at these times, see that there is a bowl of fresh milk or barley water constantly near, and if the patient is unable to lap, the liquid must be administered to him at intervals. In all cases of lung trouble, or for any sort of chill, or collapse, I immediately put the patient in a flannel jacket lined with Thermogene wool. It has an extraordinary warming and comforting effect upon sick animals, and seems to draw out the pain in a wonderful way.

BRONCHITIS.

There are few illnesses more distressing to a dog than bronchitis, and especially when it assumes a chronic form. The first symptoms are a dry and hot nose, short, hard, intermittent cough, which assumes a peculiar rattling sound, laborious breathing, eyes inflamed, fever, and loss of appetite.

As soon as the trouble is diagnosed, remove the invalid to comfortable quarters, which must be warm, yet well ventilated. A kettle, with long spout so arranged that the steam is broadly distributed, should be kept boiling in the room, as this assists the breathing, a dessert-spoonful of eucalyptus oil being added to the water. A flannel jacket (see last chapter) should immediately be placed on the dog, and his temperature taken. If the fever is over $102\frac{1}{2}$ give $\frac{1}{2}$ grains of Aspirin every four hours (see " Fever "). Rub the throat and chest twice a day with slightly warmed camphorated oil. If the cough becomes distressing, Cough Mixture should be given. A mild laxative I also recommend. The food should be tempting. Especially dainty dishes and the proper food for invalids will be found under their own heading.

COUGHS AND COLDS.

For an ordinary cough give one-half teaspoonful of the following three times a day :—Cough Mixture : Spirits of camphor, 1 dram ; paregoric elixir, 2 drams ; syrup of squills, 6 drams ; honey, 1 tablespoonful, or else Veno's cough mixture as used for children.

If the cough becomes very troublesome and throat sore, a small quantity of melted gum arabic may be given internally. It forms a coating over the irritated parts of the throat, and greatly allays the pain.

Catarrh, or cold in the head, is very contagious, therefore affected animals should always be isolated and on no account be allowed to associate with old dogs, who suffer intensely when attacked by this malady, which, with them, not infrequently assumes a chronic form or develops into asthma. The primary symptoms are shivering, violent sneezing, extreme thirst and running from the eyes and nose. Fever is also usually an accompaniment and as the symptoms are almost identical with those of distemper, it is very easy to mistake them for that disease. Until you feel perfectly sure that the case is merely a cold and not distemper, it is wise to be on the safe side and give glycerine of carbolic (for prescription, see " Distemper ") night and morning. It cannot possibly do any harm, in fact I consider it of great value in all serious illness, as it keeps the dog's internal economy in a thoroughly disinfected state, and thus in many instances staves off a severe attack. I am not fond of using much medicine in these cases, and unless the dog is really very ill I believe that careful nursing, a good deal of coddling, and plenty of nourishment, will do more good than all the drugs in the chemist's shop. The patient must, of course, be kept dry and warm, and not allowed to go out for exercise if the air is chilly. Should necessity demand, the eyes and nose must be carefully bathed in warm water, while if the nostrils become blocked, a little vaseline well rubbed into them will be found beneficial. If there is a rise in temperature, fever medicine should be administered, and in all cases the bowels well looked to. For catarrh in a mild form, and where there is not much fever, ten to twenty drops of sweet spirits of nitre in a teaspoonful of water given once a day is very successful. It acts upon the bladder, and reduces the fever in that way.

In obstinate cases one to two grains of quinine should be given, as it is especially helpful in reducing fever. This should be done at night and patient immediately put to bed and kept warm. Other remedies are frequently prescribed, but I have never found them necessary. By treating the patient thus, and by paying strict attention to dietary and general comfort, the disorder will soon yield.

PNEUMONIA.

The causes producing pneumonia or inflammation of the lungs generally arise from a chill or exposure to severe cold, but sometimes it exists as a complication of distemper. The animal does not lie down, but usually assumes a sitting posture, his breathing is rapid and oppressed, and he is unable to expand his lungs. By placing your ear at the side of the chest you can detect a grating sound within, peculiar to pneumonia, and the eyes are very much inflamed. Medicines are of a secondary consideration in this malady, and though fever mixture must, of course, be given, careful nursing is the chief point, for without it the dog's chances of recovery are nil. I have the greatest faith in a good nurse, and the poor little invalid does so appreciate having someone with him all the time, being petted, talked to and coddled, and made to feel that it is better to live than to die. He should be kept in a bright, well-ventilated room (pure air being essential), and must wear the flannel jacket (described under " Distemper ") from the very first. If the fever is over 102½, it must be taken in hand at once (see chapter on " Fever.") In severe attacks the pulse is often weak and temperature below normal, and as this condition signifies sinking, stimulants should be at once administered to encourage the pulse to a healthier action. My favourite prescription for this is Nux Vomica, 2 drops, Brandy, 4 drops ; dose, 6 drops in a tea-spoonful of water given every four hours after food. It is a wonderful heart stimulant, and seems to revive dogs when they appear to have utterly collapsed. It must be remembered, however, that Nux Vomica should only be given after food. To relieve the breathing poultices should be applied to the chest and sides (see " Pleurisy"). As the disease progresses, the extremities frequently become deathly cold. In such cases the patient should be rolled in Thermogene wool or placed in the folds of a soft, warm blanket under which is a large hot-water bottle. Give the most nourishing food, for this a particularly weakening illness, and you must do all in your power to keep up the invalid's strength. If there is much fever give Brand's essence of beef. The white of an egg beaten up in milk, Benger's, Malted Milk, or Beef Peptonoids, and no solid food till fever has abated. On no account expose him to the open air until he has fully recovered, or a relapse with disastrous effects may follow.

FEVER.

In case of illness, where fever is suspected, the temperature of the dog should at once be taken, and should the reading be above 102½ (101 being the normal temperature of the healthy dog, per rectum), prompt measures should be taken to cure it.

To begin with give half a 5-grain Aspirin tablet every four hours. The action of this drug is wonderfully quick as a rule, but it is apt to have a lowering effect upon the patient, so must not be continued for more than a couple of days at a time. I have also found Shirley's Quinine Tonic Pills excellent for reducing fever. The dose is half a pill three times a day, or else Homeopathic Aconite, dose from three to five drops every four hours. I mention several different medicines as the same thing does not suit all dogs. I unhesitatingly recommend, in cases of sustained high fever, the use of an alcohol bandage, as powerful fever mixtures are most lowering to the system and cannot be repeated often, with safety to the patient. The bandage, owing to the alcohol being absorbed through the skin, has a stimulating effect and reduces the fever gradually. To make the bandage, procure several long strips of flannel, saturate them with the best alcohol, and wrap round the dog's body. Cover the bandage with a piece of oilskin, to prevent his bed getting wet and also to check the evaporation of the spirit. Apply a fresh bandage as soon as the previous one is dry. In very mild cases of fever, where no specific disease is the cause, a mild purgative, such as a dose of liquid paraffin, will frequently prove effectual, or ten to twenty drops of sweet spirits of nitre in a teaspoonful of water given twice a day.

In all cases of fever the food must be carefully regulated, be of a light nature, and given often, in small quantities.

OPHTHALMIA.

Ophthalmia may be defined as an inflammation of the membrane covering the eyeball and the inner lining of the eyelid, usually caused by contagion, external injuries, or cold. The symptoms are a watery discharge, a dull cloudy appearance of the eye, and general inflammation. Ulceration follows, and a white film covers the eye, causing the animal partial blindness.

The treatment of ophthalmia is, as a rule, most tedious, requiring great patience and care, and no time should be lost after the symptoms are detected. Bathe the eyes several times a day with warm water, in which a good pinch of Boracic Crystals has been dissolved, using a number of small pieces of absorbent cotton wool, *and never the same piece twice* ; then by means of an eye dropper apply two or three drops of eye lotion as given below. The eye drops should always be slightly warmed before use, as the shock of anything cold is very bad for an inflamed eye.

It is best also, when bathing the eye, to draw out the under lid so that the warm Boracic Acid solution may be squeezed into the cavity and held there for a few seconds. In this way it will completely cover the eyeball, and will wash out any thick discharge which may have accumulated. The under lid should be drawn out in the same way when eye drops are applied, and the drops allowed to cover the eyeball for a minute or two. The eye itself is very tender at such times so it should be wiped as little as possible.

Eye lotion : Cocaine Hydro-Chlor., 2 grains; Ac. Boric, 5 grains ; Aq. Rosai, 2 drams ; Aq. Dist., 1 oz.

I have made a special study of the eyes and have used the eye lotion (which is entirely my own prescription) for years with simply phenomenal success.

For any sort of inflammation of the eye, the lotion can also be used, and I consider it a good plan always to have some on hand, otherwise delays may ensue and much valuable time be lost. A dog suffering from ophthalmia should be kept in a darkish place and fed on specially nourishing food, as the great pain accompanying the complaint is apt to cause considerable weakness. If bad ulceration of the cornea is present, insert into the eye at bedtime a piece the size of a small pea of the following ointment : R. Ung. Hydt. Flav., 3 grains, in addition to using the eye drops through the day.

WORMS.

Very few people seem to realize the enormous number of puppies which die every year from worms (far more than from the dreaded disease, distemper), or that in thousamds of cases they might have been saved. The good old saying that " an ounce of prevention is worth a pound of cure " is very appropriate in this instance. It is far easier to prevent puppies having worms than to rid them of these pests, when once they get a firm hold on the unfortunate infants. I am going to start at the very beginning and explain just how I should advise my readers to tackle this serious trouble.

In the first place, all adult dogs should be dosed three or four times a year for worms, even if there is no direct evidence of their presence. If the mother is free from these pests, the chance of her puppies having them to any extent is almost nil. She should be wormed before being mated, and if necessary afterwards. It is perfectly safe to give worm medicine to a bitch from two to four weeks after she had been bred. Many people do not know this. Then again just before the bitch is due to whelp her breasts should be very thoroughly washed with a rather strong solution of Lysol and warm water, and all crusts adhering to the teats picked off. This will remove worm lava, which, if left, will be sucked in by the puppies, and start immediate trouble. Dogs suffering from worms seldom thrive. Their breath is usually offensive, coat harsh, and general condition bad. They often have enormous appetites but their food does not nourish them. Eczema is also very common in such cases. Worms frequently cause paralysis in puppies ; their stomach is distended sometimes to an extraordinary size and very hard, and there is usually more or less diarrhoea. I do not advise dosing very young puppies, worm medicines have killed far more than they have ever cured.   It stands to reason that any drug strong enough to destroy these tough-skinned parasites, is going to seriously affect the delicate membrane lining the intestines and stomach, and in many cases it will set up acute gastritis or other intestinal complications. What one must do is to feed the puppy on the best and most nourishing of food and tone up his system so that when he is four or five months old he will be strong enough to stand the dosing.   When very young puppies die of worms it will be found in nine cases out of ten that their dam was below par when they were born, underfed, and, to put it plainly, in no condition to breed from.

People have only themselves to blame when this occurs, and it will not occur if the precautions I have mentioned are carried out and only really healthy animals bred from.   When first dosing puppies, personally, I always use a preparation called Ruby, and later on Shirley's Toy Dog Pills, or else Geo. Welch's Toy Dog Pills.   They are both perfectly safe to give, and most effective.   For breeders who do not live in England and are unable to obtain the above, the following is excellent, and should be given twice a week before food :

PRESCRIPTION FOR WORM MIXTURE IN PUPPIES—Santonine, 1 scruple ; Liquor Senna Dulc., 1 oz. ; Glycerine, ½ oz. ; Syrup Aniseed, 3½ ozs.   Mix well and shake before giving.   Dose : For small puppies such as Pekingese or Toy Spaniels, when 6 weeks old, 15 drops. Increase as the puppies get older.

For grown toy dogs I prefer the well-known Freeman's Tape Worm Gelatine Capsules, they are " death " to any kind of worm, and do not distress even the smallest or most delicate of dogs.   They are put up in two sizes, A (for dogs from 6 to 8 lbs.) and, B (for dogs from 3 to 5 lbs.   I mention these capsules as I have used them successfully for many years and because it is so risky for the novice to give unknown and indiscriminative quack mixtures, for these kill more puppies than they cure.

It is *very* important that cod liver oil or liquid paraffin should be given every night for at least a week before the worm medicine is administered (dose : a dessertspoonful for adults and half the quantity for puppies).   Oil paves the way to success for any sort of oil is distasteful to worms.   It helps to make them loosen their hold on the dog so that when the actual vermifuge is given they come away quite easily, having been more or less dislodged by the constant presence of oil in the stomach and bowels.   I have, in fact, known quantities of worms expelled by the use of oil only, and I am sure that if it was generally known what an enormous help it is in getting rid of these pests it would be more frequently used. Castor oil is sometimes given shortly after a worm pill, but it very often upsets small or delicate dogs and makes them sick, thus doing away with the object of the vermifuge. Cod liver oil never does this, in fact most dogs like it and lick it from a spoon, and it is perfectly harmless.

Whilst on the subject of castor oil, I might mention here that this can be bought in gelatine capsule form, and it is a very good idea to use it in this form should castor oil be required. It is very easy to give in capsules, and does not get all over the dog's coat, which is so often the case if the liquid is used.

To return to the dosing. The last meal (which should be a small and sloppy one) must not be given later than 4 o'clock the day before the dose is administered, the cod liver oil given as usual in the evening, and the pills on an empty stomach the first thing next morning. No food should be given for at least two hours afterwards, and then only a warm sloppy mixture, or milk, and no solid food for 24 hours.

There are various kinds of worms which may be roughly classified as round and tape worms. The former are more frequently found in puppies. They resemble pieces of thin twine from $1\frac{1}{2}$ to 2 inches long, and are pointed at each end. The presence of tape worm may be detected by small segments of the worm, which look like pieces of dried rice and are usually found underneath the tail or adhering to the rectum Round worms are comparatively easy to get rid of, but not so the tape worm, he is a troublesome customer, and the dog will require many doses before he is effectually dislodged.

There is a very serious and often fatal disease which may be contracted by human beings if they should happen to swallow the egg or lava of a tape worm which forms a cyst or bladder worm in the liver. If tape worm lava can be transmitted to human beings in this way, just think how very easy it must be to pass it on from one dog to the other, and how very foolish it is for people owning dogs to neglect dosing them regularly and systematically for worms.

GASTRITIS (ACUTE).

This trouble is not usually difficult to deal with if taken in time, but, if neglected, may terminate fatally in a very few days. The first symptoms are loss of appetite, restlessness, vomiting and diarrhoea, and in its early stages it is almost impossible to determine whether the patient is in for an attack of ordinary Gastritis, a chill on the liver or Gastro Enteritis (otherwise Stuttgart Distemper), a most infectious and dangerous malady, so it is always best to be on the safe side and isolate

I

him at once. The treatment for these three ailments is much the same, but with common Gastritis the patient is extremely thirsty and we do not get much fever, whereas with both of the other troubles I have mentioned there is always a fever, and sometimes a very high fever, which must be taken in hand immediately. For this I recommend one half of a 5-grain Aspirin tablet given night and morning, and the following days continue with Shirley's Quinine Tonic Pills (see " Distemper.") In this as in practically all other serious troubles a Thermogene wool jacket should be put on the patient at once (see chapter on " Nursing ") and my own pet preparation of Bismuth and Bi-carbonate of Soda given to relieve the sickness and check diarrhoea. Proportion : 1 part of Bi-carb. to 2 of Bismuth ; dose, as much as will lie on a 6d. piece, every 4 hours. I might say here that this can be given for any gastric or stomach troubles. It is perfectly safe to give and its action is simply wonderful. I have known it to stop vomiting when every other thing had failed. If, however, it does fail, the dog's inside must be given a complete rest. To persistently give food when a dog is vomiting is most unwise, although an ignorant person might do so with the idea of keeping up his strength. If the dog's stomach cannot retain food, mouth feeding must be stopped and you must rely solely upon Peptonised Beef suppositories, one of which can be gently pressed up into the rectum every three hours. Milk, mixed with starch and a small proportion of melted Gum Arabic can also be injected into the bowels as an alternative. When the sickness has stopped food may again be given by the mouth in infinitesimal quantities to begin with, and very gradually increased. To give too much as a start will only upset the dog's internal economy again. It is much better to err on the safe side and give too little. He will be very weak if the vomiting has been severe, and one is often tempted to overdo the feeding up, so I want to make it clear that very, very little should be allowed at first. I prefer boiled milk, in which a pinch of raw arrowroot and the white of an egg, and a few grains of melted Gum Arabic is mixed. The action of the Gum Arabic is wonderfully soothing to an exhausted stomach as it creates a false coating, and in that way assists the much-strained tissues to build up again, it also has a very binding effect upon the bowels. Other good food is Peptonised Beef or chicken jelly, Beef Peptonoids and Horlick's Malted Milk, and when the convalescent stage is reached, scraped raw beef or mutton, minced chicken and the various foods mentioned under Invalid Feeding will restore him to strength again, better than anything else.

I have mentioned above that extreme thirst is one of the most marked symptoms of acute Gastritis, and, unfortunately, very little can be done at first to relieve it, because the dog must not be given any water at all to drink until the sickness has completely stopped. He may have a teaspoonful of Vichy water occasionally, or better still, a small piece of ice to lick from time to time, but, disastrous results will follow if he is allowed to overload his stomach with cold water.

The patient must be kept in an even temperature and on no account be allowed out of doors or to lie about where he might get chilled. He must have a snug bed to lie in, which should be absolutely draught-proof. The Thermogene wool jacket will relieve the pain caused by inflammation in the stomach.

INFLUENZA (SEPTIC).

A new disease about which very little is known at the moment, but it seems to be much the same as the human Influenza which was raging in Europe (and for that matter in most parts of the world) in 1917 and 1918. The first symptoms are often mistaken for those of Distemper, but in most cases there is none of that never-to-be-forgotten smell peculiar to Distemper. The temperature is very erratic. Normal one day, high the next, and possibly sub-normal later on. I dread the sub-normal most of all, as it points to septic trouble, but the high temperature is also a warning, and a forerunner of Pneumonia. Some dogs start with a husky cough and shivering, some with sickness and diarrhoea, but the worst form is when the lungs are affected.

I regret to say that the mortality is very great in these cases, and the only hope is to relieve the congestion of the lungs in its very early stages, for as with human beings the poison or septic complications are so quick in their development that you must tackle them from the very beginning if you are to meet with success. When Influenza is suspected the first thing to be done is to remove the dog to a bright cheerful room, make him as comfortable as possible, take his temperature, sew him into a flannel jacket lined with Thermogene wool and await developments. Influenza is horribly contagious, and a dog suffering from it should be isolated at once, and kept in strict quarantine. They should be treated much the same as if they had Distemper. In many cases the attack may be a light one, and the patient will scarcely go off his food at all, but if they have it in the septic form, the nurse will have her work cut out to save them.

The early symptoms of Pneumonia are usually a rise of temperature, followed by that peculiar rapid and oppressed breathing which an experienced person dreads, and knows only too well. A sustained high fever is very weakening, and on no account must be allowed to run on unchecked. To reduce the fever give half a 5-grain Aspirin tablet every four hours. I might mention here, however, that Aspirin has rather a lowering effect so you should not continue it for more than a couple of days at a time. It is a wonderful drug when carefully used, but should it fail to bring down the temperature you must continue with Shirley's Quinine Tonic Pills (dose : half to one pill every four hours). The quinine is very helpful in all cases of Influenza, and it is about the only medicine I care to prescribe for this trouble. Half a pill can be safely given twice a day all through an attack, but not, of course, in conjunction with Aspirin.

To relieve the breathing shave every atom of hair from the region of both lungs, then rub well into the skin a patent medicine called Iodex. It is most satisfactory stuff to use, because it does not distress the patient in the slightest degree, is easily applied, and perfectly safe. Iodex should not be applied oftener than once a day as too much of it will soon make the skin tender. It is, in fact, best only to apply it every second day except in bad cases. Antifrogistine is another very fine thing to reduce inflammation of the lungs (see Pleurisy), but it is much more difficult to apply, and may upset the dog a good deal if put on too hot. Linseed poultices are also good, but they should only be used by an expert, as they must be applied in quick rotation, otherwise the danger of cold is very great indeed, and for this reason I cannot recommend them. The Iodex is an excellent substitute and can do no harm.

If the cough is troublesome Veno's Cough Mixture (as given to children) is excellent and a teaspoonful of melted gum arabic is also most soothing. The great thing in these cases is to make the dog comfortable, see that his room is well ventilated, yet free from draughts, and feed him on the best and most easily digested food. I am very fond of lightly roasted chicken or mutton, and would give it in small quantities provided the dog will take it himself, even if he has a fever, for it is absolutely necessary to keep up the patient's strength in septic cases, and dogs very quickly tire of a purely milk diet, which is all many people will allow if there is a fever. Horlick's malted milk tablets are also A1 at this time. It should always be remembered that a teaspoonful of food taken voluntarily does more good than a tablespoonful given forcibly. In order to successfully treat the various complications of Influenza which may occur, I refer my reader to the chapters on Gastritis, Distemper, Pneumonia, Diarrhoea, Coughs and Colds and Ophthalmia.

.

FOR ALL SMALL BREEDS
OLD CALABAR
"MIDGETS"

KEEP YOUR PETS IN HEALTH AND CONDITION.

OF ALL DEALERS, OR FROM

OLD CALABAR, LTD., LIVERPOOL.

KWAI-KWAI OF EGHAM.

THE ASHTON-MORE PEKINGESE
The Property of Lieut.-Col. and Mrs. A. M. RAYMOND-MALLOCK, at 2, Preston Park Avenue, Brighton. Phone Preston 3561.

Photo]   *[Fall*

Head Study of ASHTON-MORE WEN-CHU.

	Stud Fees.		
ASHTON-MORE WEN CHU			
Golden Fawn, by Nanking Wen-Chu	£10	10	0
ASHTON-MORE CHU-CHI			
Winner of 7 first prizes at his first show	£10	10	0
ASHTON-MORE FOO-KWAI			
Golden "Sun Dog," by Kwai-Kwai of Egham, Winner of 70 prizes	£10	10	0
ASHTON-MORE SHA-TSU			
Wolf Sable, by Sutherland Av. Sha-Tsu	£5	5	0
ASHTON-MORE PAO-CHU			
Small Red Brindle, with a wonderful muzzle ...	£5	5	0
ASHTON-MORE HENI-SU			
Fawn, winner of 5 first prizes at his two first shows	£5	5	0
ASHTON-MORE FO-CHU			
Bright red, by Remenham Riondello	£3	3	0
ASHTON-MORE YUNG MOSHO			
Light red, siring big litters of lovely puppies ...	£3	3	0

For illustrations of above see chapter on Pekingese.

THE ASHTON-MORE PEKINGESE

The Property of Lieut.-Col. and Mrs. A. M. RAYMOND-MALLOCK,
at 2, Preston Park Avenue, Brighton.   Phone Preston 3561.

oto]

ASHTON-MORE WEN-CHU,
One of the most perfect Pekingese in existence.

Dogs from these Kennels and their progeny have won
hundreds of prizes and many championships.

PUPPIES, SHOW AND BREEDING STOCK USUALLY FOR SALE.

NANKING WEN-CHU. Fee 20 Guineas.

NANKING WEN-TU. Fee 15 Guineas.

NANKING WENTI-TU. Fee 10 Guineas.

NANKING YUNG-FO. Fee 5 Guineas.

NANKING WAI-JEN. Fee 7 Guineas.

NANKING YOAN-FAN. Fee 7 Guineas.

ROGERS'
Warm Puppy Brooder.

A Receptacle for Rearing PUPPIES FROM BIRTH.

Also Weakly and Bad Doers which are brought up by Hand Feeding.

Will keep as a Warm Nest for 12hrs. with Hot Water only. The Puppies sleeping in a Removable Nest do not come in contact with heated sides of Brooder.

Royal Letters British Patent No. 777/11.   Also Patented in U.S., America.

A BOON TO BREEDERS.

FOSTER BITCHES superseded ;   besides the risk of strange bitches not taking to a litter.   Also chances of infection from unknown kennels.   No matter of what breed, there are always weakly ones that get pushed out in the cold, and in the Inventor's experience get starved and die off—in many cases the pick of the litter.   Then, again, milk running short with the bitch, which necessitates hand feeding.   Hence the requirement of the PATENT WARM BROODER to carry them through the day and night for warmth.   The PATENT WARM BROODER can easily be carried from one room to another, so that the puppies are under the care of the attendant for feeding purposes.

15in. Brooder, inside measurement, for Pekingese,

Japanese, etc.	...	...	...	...	£3	15	0

18in. do., do., for Terriers, Pugs and the like ...   5   0   0
21in. do., do., for Bull Pups, Bloodhounds, etc. ...   6 10   0

N.B.—Most Breeders of Toys use the 18in. Brooder as a warm receptacle for both Mother and Puppies.   All sizes can be used for keeping the newly-born Puppies warm until the mother has finished whelping.

Testimonial from a High-Class Pomeranian Breeder with a Rogers' Patent Warm Puppy Brooder.

Kirk-Langley, Derby.

DEAR SIR,—I have found your Puppy Brooder a great success.   A very small Pom Bitch of mine had two pups, one of which, on going to the kennels, I picked up thinking it was dead ; it was, as far as I could see, lifeless, and the other was nearly as bad.   I put the mother and the two pups into the brooder, as soon as it could be filled with hot water, and both the pups revived and were reared to maturity.   This, I am sure, is entirely due to the fact of the pups being surrounded with warmth when in the Brooder, as they were in an unheated out-door kennel.—Yours faithfully, Mrs. A. K. GOODALL-COPESTAKE.

Also highly recommended by Mrs. L. C. RAYMOND-MALLOCK.

E. E. ROGERS, Patentee and Sole Manufacturer,
FOUR OAKS, Warwickshire, England.

Burton-on-Dee Kennels.

PHILIP OF BURTON-ON-DEE
(Championship Winner).

A noseless red brindle son of LAUREL OF LANG. PHILIP is siring exceptional puppies excelling in flatness of face, bone and front.

Fee 6 Guineas.

DIMBIE OF BURTON-ON-DEE (sire Ch. Chinly Chog). **Fee 5 Gns.**
DIMBIE OF HARTLEBURY (by Dimbie of Burton-on-Dee), ,, **5 Gns.**
JOSS OF BURTON-ON-DEE (by Dimbie of Burton-on-Dee). ,, **5 Gns.**
PAUL OF BURTON-ON-DEE (by Sumie of Lang). ,, **5 Gns.**
FEATHER OF BURTON-ON-DEE (by Joss of Burton-on-Dee) ,, **4 Gns.**
BUFFY OF BURTON-ON-DEE (by Patsee of Kuen Lun). ., **4 Gns.**

All these dogs possess very short faces, flat skulls, good bone and coats. Good puppies by them are nearly always for sale.

Mrs. PATRICK MORRELL, Burton Vicarage, Neston, Birkenhead.

THE LUTONIA PEKINGESE (Registered Prefix).

LUTONIA CH-IEN
(At 18 months old. Winner at open shows).

Stud Dogs include

LUTONIA YUAN
(Son of Ch. Lyncroft Chops).
Fee 2 guineas.

LUTONIA CH-IEN
(Son of Ch. Nanking Wenti).
Fee 3 guineas.

LUTONIA WENTI
(Grandson of Ch. Nanking
Wenti). Fee 3 guineas.

*All are typical short faced
specimens and siring flat faced
puppies.*

Photo booklet from **Mrs.
Shepherd, Pekin, Clarendon
Road, Luton, Beds.**

SUNDEN TSING-TAO,
Owned and bred by **Miss Daubeny, South Bersted, Bognor, Sussex.**

Sunden Tsing-Tao has won many prizes at the leading shows, including Reserve Championship. At Stud, fee, **20 Guineas.** His home bred winning sons are " Kio," London ; "Ticker Toe Toy F.,"Ryde, the sensational South American winner; " Dogo of Ashcroft " ; also " Yu Wang of Frere," " Tzi-an," and " Judy of Sherhill."

McDOUGALL'S
(PATENT)
KUR-MANGE
NON-POISONOUS   NON-CARBOLIC

DESTROYS LICE, FLEAS AND OTHER PARASITES.

ASHTON-MORE KWAI-KWAI.

KUR-MANGE is regularly used in the "ASHTON-MORE" and other well-known Kennels, and is considered invaluable by numerous Dog Owners throughout the Country.

Descriptive Leaflet sent on application.

66-68, PORT ST., MANCHESTER.

McDOUGALL'S
(PATENT)
KUR-MANGE
NON-POISONOUS   **NON-CARBOLIC**

A CERTAIN REMEDY FOR PARASITIC MANGE AND RINGWORM.

ASHTON-MORE FOO-KWAI (as a Puppy).

KUR-MANGE improves the Coat, and keeps the Skin in a Clean and Healthy Condition.

Sold in 8oz. Packets and 7lb. Tins.   From all leading Chemists.

Sole Manufacturers :

McDOUGALL BROS., LTD.,

Mrs. ASHTON CROSS'S PEKINGESE.

At Beech Hill, Mayford, Woking.   Tel. Woking 542.

Mrs. Ashton Cross has a few really first class show specimens, dogs. and bitches, for sale.   Some big winners and others fit for show in the highest competition, but ineligible in England.   Brood bitches from **15** guineas.   She has also a number of wonderful little sleeve specimens, sound and healthy and 3lbs. weight.   Moderate prices.

CHUTY-TOO OF ALDERBOURNE.

Chuty-Too, of Alderbourne, shown seven times in 1920, and winner at those shows of 55 First and Special Prizes, Championship and Pierpoint Moxom Cup.   Siring large litters of winning puppies.

Mrs. Ashton Cross will be pleased to show these dogs to anyone interested in Pekingese.

Mrs. ASHTON CROSS'S PEKINGESE.

At Beech Hill, Mayford, Woking. Tel. Woking 542.

CHAMPION CHU-ERH TU OF ALDERBOURNE.

Champion Chu-erh Tu of Alderbourne, the latest Pekingese Champion. Winner of many firsts and cups at all the best shows. Sire of a large number of winners, and many exquisite puppies coming out shortly.

The Alderbourne Pekingese at Stud.

Chuty-Too of Alderbourne, Parti-colour - - -	**20** guineas
Ch. Chu-erh Tu of Alderbourne, red parti-colour -	**15** guineas
Ch. Tien Joss of Greystones, red - - -	**15** guineas
Tai-Choo of Alderbourne, grey, Championship winner -	**15** guineas
Choo-Tai of Alderbourne, red, 7lbs. - - - -	**10** guineas
Prince Kang-Yi of Moor Park, red, by Ch. Chuty - -	**10** guineas
Pao-Kwai of Alderbourne, fawn, sire of winners - -	**5** guineas
Wen-Tu of Alderbourne, red, by Wen-Ti - - -	**5** guineas
Nickie of Alderbourne, red colour, by Chu-erh Tu -	**5** guineas
Tsing-Chu of Alderbourne, red parti-colour - -	**5** guineas
Too-Ki of Alderbourne, grey, by Chuty-Too - -	**3** guineas
Chow-Chu of Moor Park, red, 7lbs. - - - -	**3** guineas

Mrs. Calley's Pekingese.

The Greatest Winning Pekingese ever bred. Holder of the Record Number of Championships (20) for this breed, besides innumerable other prizes.

CH. KOTZU OF BURDEROP.

Taken at 9 months. A Winner every time shown, and by the time she was 16 months old had taken 4 Reserve Championships and 45 First and Special Prizes, including 6 Challenge Cups at the Chief Shows.

MOUSIE OF BURDEROP.

Address : BURDEROP PARK, SWINDON.

Mrs. Calley's Pekingese.

By
Li of Chinatown
ex Mela.

FEE
at present,
£5 5s.

Siring Winners
in every litter,
including
MOUSIE OF
BURDEROP,
4 times Reserve
Champion be-
fore 16 months
old ;
KUAN OF
BURDEROP,
Reserve Cham-
pion, Pekingese
Club Summer
Show, 1920,
when only 17
months old,
and many
others.

YING SU OF BURDEROP.

KUAN OF BURDEROP.

By Ying Su
of Burderop,
ex Chu-Tzu
of Burderop
(by Ch. Ko-Tzu
of Burderop).

FEE
(at present)
£5 5s.

Winner of
First & Reserve
Championship
Pekingese Club.

Address : BURDEROP PARK, SWINDON.

T is an old story that Mrs. Frances Mary Weaver bred Sutherland Ouen-teu-T'ang and Champion Chu'erh, as senile decay has removed them from our midst, but it is interesting to have watched her kennel through the past 16 years, during which time the excellence of her dogs has not only been maintained but it has been greatly increased. When it is borne in mind that her breeding stock never exceeds a score and that she has never exhibited in her life, it is obvious that her success has been due solely to the quality of her dogs and her skill in the choice of mates.

Her policy of working with nothing but the finest specimens of the purest strains and rejecting anything not true to type is surely abundantly justified in the results.

Her present stud dogs are :—

SUTHERLAND AVE. SHA-TZU. One of the late Sutherland Ouen-teu-T'ang's finest grandsons. He has a wonderfully flat face with nose embedded in wrinkles. He is a profusely coated dog with short heavy-boned fore legs, which are a speciality of " The Sutherlands."

NEA SHAZA. Sha-tzu's sire, and the late Ouen's finest living son.

SUTHERLAND AVE. KWA. A red dog with practically the same points as Nea Shaza, but in miniature.

SUTHERLAND AVE. CHO. A red and white parti-colour, quite unique in his massiveness, though only a small dog.

NANKING TING and **SUTHERLAND AVE. HO.** These two seniors are too well known to need description.

Mrs. Frances Mary Weaver is always pleased to send pictures of these dogs and to show them in life by appointment at 199, Sutherland Avenue, Maida Vale, London, W.9.

CHANG-CHIO of Sunnyfields Farm.

133

CANINE DISTEMPER

ASHTON-MORE FOO-KWAI.

Inoculated as a Puppy with these Threads.   Winner of 70 prizes.
Shown extensively all over England, and has never had Distemper.

The late Prof. Woodroffe Hill's system of Protective Inoculation,
successfully practised for 30 years, and highly recommended by
Mrs. Raymond Mallock, and used for many years in her Kennels.

THE INOCULATING THREADS
(Which can be used without a Vet's. assistance),

5/- each,

CAN BE OBTAINED FROM

G. S. WOODROFFE HILL,

22, HEREFORD,

BAYSWATER, LONDON, W.

TYPICAL RED SABLE PEKINGESE,
QUIMBO OF LATCHFORD.

The property of **Mrs. L. POMFRETT, 10, Barry Street, Latchford, Warringt.on**

QUIMBO OF LATCHFORD.
(Aged 10 months).
By **Quimbo of Earlsferry and Bun-nee of Kuen-Lun.**
Born 8th September, 1919.

ONE OF CHAMPION LYNCROFT CHOP'S BEST GRANDSONS.

QUIMBO. Shaded red sable, typical face and head; shows great promise of making a perfect specimen, with an absolute flat black face, dark eyes, very short, well bowed legs, and short lion-like body and perfect tail carriage.

AT STUD. **Fee for the present, £2 2s.**

SUTHERLAND AVENUE KUANTZU.

The well known winner and sire of winners at all the leading Shows.

Red, black mask.

———

Fee 4 Gns.

BOY OF KUEN-LUN.

Sire late Patsee of Kuen-lun, ex Sutherland Avenue Chutieh (Sutherland Ouen teu T'ang). Red, black mask, absolutely "punched-in" face. Siring wonderful puppies.

———

Fee 4 Gns.

Mrs. JAMES KENWORTHY'S PEKINGESE,
at Woodleigh, Thornton, nr. Liverpool.

CHIN OF KUEN-LUN.

Sire late Patsee of Kuen-lun, ex Quilla of Kuen-lun. Well-balanced fawn brindle. Winner at Championship Shows. Sire of high quality puppies.

Fee 3 guineas.

QUIMBO OF EARLS FERRY.

Handsome red son of Ch. Lyncroft Chops, ex daughter of Ch. Nanking Wexti. Winner and sire of winners.

Fee 3 guineas.

HORLICK'S MALTED MILK
Lunch Tablets.

These delicious food tablets contain all the well-known nutritive qualities of Horlick's Malted Milk, and their distinctive natural flavour makes them acceptable to all tastes. As every particle is pure, easily digested nourishment they are most efficient in maintaining health and strength, and when travelling they are especially useful, as they may be carried very conveniently.

—— Supplied in ——
Glass Pocket Flasks—7½d. and 1/3,
and in larger bottles at 2/- & 3/6.
Of all Chemists and Stores When
ordering ask for and insist on
—— **having "HORLICK'S."** ——

HORLICK'S MALTED MILK CO., SLOUGH, BUCKS, ENGLAND.

Zelph of Ayot's Daughter, Ch. NANKING WENTI 105th.

Bitches and Dogs this type and blood.

Mrs. AMES, Welwyn, England.

Carnrick's Liquid Peptonoids

ASHTON-MORE ADONIS.

Bred by Mrs. RAYMOND MALLOCK.

Contains the real, essential nutriment—Protein and Carbo-Hydrates—derived from our principal food-stuffs — Beef, Wheat and Milk. The food-elements in "Liquid Peptonoids" are *pre-digested*, so that the nutriment afforded can be readily assimilated in conditions of disease and exhaustion when the digestive powers are in consequence weakened. **Carnrick's** "Liquid Peptonoids" is a mild stimulant, and is extremely palatable and pleasant in every way. **Carnrick's** "Liquid Peptonoids" is a most valuable *Restorative Food*, that has been used and approved by Medical Men for many years.

The Lancet writes :—"A very valuable food. . . . a very powerful and agreeable tonic and stimulant."

The Hospital : "Its most valuable feature is that clinically it has proved itself capable of absorption when everything else has been rejected by the stomach."

The properties that have made Carnrick's **" Liquid Peptonoids "** so useful in the treatment of humans make it also most effective in the dieting of our pets when sick. In conditions of digestive debility, loss of appetite, etc., it can be used with great advantage, and in Distemper it would seem to be specially useful.

A well-known Breeder writes :—" I have used it almost exclusively over and over again with excellent results for dogs suffering from Distemper."

Carnrick's "LIQUID PEPTONOIDS " can be obtained from Chemists holding a Wine Licence.

CARNRICK & CO., LTD., 183, ACTON VALE, LONDON, W.

SHERLEY'S WORM CAPSULES
for DOGS.

(OF 10lbs. WEIGHT AND OVER).

These Capsules are tasteless and odourless, and are the surest and safest remedy for expelling both Round and Tape Worms from dogs (or puppies three months old and over) weighing 10lbs. or more. They require no purgative medicine afterwards, and may be easily given wrapped up in a piece of meat, fish, &c.

Price 1/3 and 2/6.   Postage extra 1½d.

ASHTON-MORE WEN-CHU (as a Puppy).

SHERLEY'S WORM CAPSULES
for PUPPIES and TOY DOGS.

These Capsules may be safely given to the smallest and most delicate Puppies and Toy Dogs.   They are small, cleanly, tasteless, and odourless, whilst no castor oil is required before or after giving them. Puppies do not need to fast before being given them.

Price 1/3 and 2/6.   Postage extra 1½d.

A. F. SHERLEY & CO., 48, Borough High Street, London, E.C.

ASHTON-MORE PAO-KWAI.

GOOD SERVICE.

We know that the only way to get business and to keep it is by giving **PROMPT, CAREFUL** and **EFFICIENT SERVICE.** We satisfy others and will satisfy you.

CONSIGN YOUR SHIPMENTS TO US, and send Bill of Lading, Invoice, etc., together with your instructions direct to us, which will expedite the Release of the Animals from Customs Control.

We make a speciality of Clearing Dogs and other Live Stock through Customs.

ASHTON-MORE FAN-KWEI.
A well-known sleeve winner at Championship Shows.   Weight 4½lbs.   **Fee 7 Gns.**

TZU-CHU OF MOUNT RICH.
Sire Pao-Chu of Noke ex Rita of Mount Rich.   **Fee 5 Guineas.**

The MISSES KENT and LANGDON'S PEKINGESE,
At 182, Cromwell Road, S.W.

TOTO OF MOUNT RICH.
Sire Toto of Noke ex Betty of Mount Rich.
Fee, 15 Guineas.

TOTO TU OF MOUNT RICH.
Sire Toto of Mount Rich. **Fee at present, 5 Guineas.**

AT KINGSMEAD, WINDSOR (Phone Windsor 47).

HOLYWOOD LIT-ZU.

Sire Ch Nanking Wenti. Dam, Holywood Hua. Lovely small red gold bitch with absolutely squashed-in face, perfect eyes, legs, shape and feathering. Winner everywhere shown and took bitch championship at Richmond, July 6th, 1920. Born February 13th, 1917.

HOLYWOOD CHOPS.

Sire Ch. Lyncroft Chops. Dam, Destiny of Bucklands. Proved sire, gorgeous coat and feathering, bright orange red, massive bone, low to ground and perfect legs and figure. Short face. Fee for present, £3 3s.

TU SING OF GREYSTONES.

Reared on Virol.

Miss HOUSTON, St. Davids, Greystones, Co. Wicklow, says :—

" I have used Virol now for some time in my large kennel of Pekingese ; every puppy is reared on it. I recommend Virol to everyone who has a small puppy."

Virol stimulates the protective cells of the blood against the germs of disease, an important factor in distemper. It feeds the tissues of the body and strengthens the bones. Virol is used by all the principal dog breeders in the country.

In Jars, 1/3, 2/- and 3 9, Half-Gallons, 15/-.

VIROL

Virol Limited, 148-166, Old Street, London, E.C.1.

HOLYWOOD HOP-HO.
By **H. Mosho** and **Holywood Flicka**.
A magnificient young dog, with tremendous coat, short face, good eyes, very low to ground and very heavy bone.

HOLYWOOD WEN-CHU.
By **Nanking Wen-Chu** and **Pekelan Zenwu**.
Splendid young fawn brindle dog, magnificent shape, bone, eyes and extra short face. Tail carriage perfect.

HOLYWOOD MOSHO.

Sire, Ch. Nanking Wenti.   Dam, Holywood Dinkie, by Ch. Chinky Chogs, a lovely small fawn dog, 8lbs. weight, sire of exquisite puppies.   **Stud fee, £5 5s.**

HOLYWOOD TIEN-HOW.

Cream coloured bitch by Ashton-More Fo and Mrs. Robinson's Scamp.   Born June 8th, 1916; gorgeous feathering and huge dark eyes and absolutely squashed face.

147

THE GREATEST TONIC OF THE DAY.

J. D. T.

Absolutely unrivalled for obtaining Show Condition.

AS USED IN THE WINNING KENNELS OF THIS YEAR.

There is nothing like it for producing BONE, rich blood and nervous energy.

For puppies, bitches and stud dogs it is a genuine body builder without throwing undue strain on the nervous system.

By using it you will give your dog every chance.

Testimonials and repeat orders galore.

Post free 5s. 6d. per bottle.

AN EFFECTIVE SKIN LOTION.

J. S. L.

For Mange (all kinds), Eczema and any skin disease.

Non-greasy and does not stain the coat.

Non-poisonous.

Post free 3s. and 5s. 6d. per bottle.

"J" Brand WORM OIL.

This oil by regular use acts as a gentle aperient and at the same time restores the intestines to a healthy condition.

It is a valuable remedy rendering the intestinal tracts too healthy for worms to obtain a hold. It is therefore an exceedingly valuable medicine because its regular use frees the dog from worms *and it does not upset the system.*

For Toy Dogs it is particularly *safe* and reliable.

In bottles 2s. 6d. and 5s. post free.

"J" Brand COAT OIL.

(Antiseptic) for promoting the growth of hair of the Dog.

This oil is used by most of the successful exhibition owners of the day.

As a dressing it is invaluable. Being antiseptic it keeps the coat sweet and clean and free from insects.

In bottles 2s. 6d. and 5s. post free.

J. M. JOHNSON, M.P.S., *Veterinary Chemist,*
72, Carless Avenue, Harborne, BIRMINGHAM.

Mrs. MILES' PEKINGESE

AT

"THE AVIARIES," CHICHESTER.

At stud, PETERKIN TEE, a beautiful little dog, by SUTHERLAND AVENUE SINE BAH.

Red, black mask, short face, well bowed, low and cobby, good coat, well carried plume and lovely figure; 5½lbs. Proved sire of lovely black-masked Puppies. Fee 3 Guineas.

SMALL BITCHES ONLY RECEIVED.

PUPPIES USUALLY FOR SALE.

ASHTON-MORE NAN-TYE.

HARTLEBURY JOHN O' DREAMS, bright red with black mask. Aged 7 months. Son of Yuan of Hartlebury. Winner at his first show (Llanrust), of two First prizes, two Seconds and two Specials.

HARTLEBURY JOHN O' DREAMS.

Please note that **Mrs. H. C. Holder** is moving from Hartlebury, and that her new address is **Linden Hill, Twyford, Berks.**

THE HARTLEBURY PEKINGESE.

YUAN OF HARTLEBURY, bright red, son of T'san Pam of Chinatown.
Winner of many Firsts and Specials for best in show. Fee
10 Guineas to approved Bitches.

POO-GEE OF HARTLEBURY, son of Yuan and litter brother to
John o' Dreams. Palest fawn with black mask.

Please note that **Mrs. H. C. Holder** is moving from Hartlebury, and
that her new address is **Lidnen Hill, Twyford, Berks.**

THE FRERE PEKINGESE.

The Property of Mrs. **R. A. GIBBONS**, at 29, Cadogan Place, S.W. 11.
Phone Victoria 3660.

YÜ TING OF FRERE

Best young son of Ch. Broadoak Beetle living. Dam Palace T'sun,
b. of Ch. Chuty of Alderbourne, ex Sho, b. of Ch. Goodwood Lo,
ex Ch. Gia-Gia.

Fee, **Ten Guineas.**

Fawn, dense black mask. Weight 8lbs.

Breeder - **Mrs. R. A. GIBBONS.**

THE FRERE PEKINGESE.

The Property of Mrs. R. A. GIBBONS, at 29, Cadogan Place, S.W. 11.
Phone Victoria 3660.

MONGOL DAH-RUN

Red and White parti, son of Major Stafford Cox's imported dog,
Mongol Yaou Fing.   Dam, Wei-Hai-Wei of Craiglea.   Proud sire of
lovely puppies.

Fee, for a short time only, **Six Guineas.**

ALSO

YÜ WHANG OF FRERE

Bright Red.   Sire, Sundru Tsing Tao.   Dam by Chin Tzun of Vassia.
Fee, **Seven Guineas.**

THE FRERE PEKINGESE.

The Property of Mrs. R. A. GIBBONS, at 29, Cadogan Place, S.W. 11.
Phone Victoria 3660.

TIEN-WHAH OF FRERE, Red, black shadings ; born Jan. 31st, 1919. Sire, Mongol
Yaou Fing (imported); dam,Marku,b.of Palace Cheu Tao. **Breeder,Mrs.R.A. GIBBONS.**

ANITA OF FRERE, Grey brindle, dense black mask. Sire the late Chillemel Lu-
Lu ; Dam, Alresford Mimosa, b. of S-av.Vue. **Breeder, Mrs. R. A. GIBBONS.**

Miss GRIFFITHS' "LANG" KENNEL OF PEKINGESE.
At 8, Rose Mount, Oxton, Birkenhead.

SUNNIE OF LANG (By Laurel of Lang).

Sunnie is a winner, and sire of many winners including Paul of Burton on Dee, and Monica of Burton on Dee (both in one litter) ; Ti Pai Sun of Westlecott, Sunlocks of Lang and Bobbie of Lang. **Fee 4 Guineas.**

SUNLOCKS OF LANG at 5 months. Bred by Miss Griffiths.

E-WO T'U.

A handsome Grey Brindle, good all round, has a particularly nice expression, smart carriage and action. Sires small and lovely puppies, who are noseless and inherit his big eyes, strong underjaw and beautiful coat. Weight about 8lbs. Fee 10 Guineas. Date of Birth, 1915.

E-WO MOLO-MAN

A jet black dog. This is a compact little miniature, possessing a marvellous head and facial properties, level mouth and absolutely noseless, has good bone, carriage and action. Sires small and exquisite puppies, usually black, noseless and with his characteristics. Those desiring to breed really good sound Blacks

should bear him in mind. Fee 10 Guineas. Weight about 6½lbs. Date of Birth, 1915.

These dogs are out of a very beautiful black bitch (Sleeve specimen), that Mrs. Jardine Gresson brought from Pekin in 1912 and who never had a bad puppy. Most of Mrs. Gresson's stock are descended from this strain.

Mrs. R. MORREL'S TAN SHI OF ALDERBOURNE. Winner 1st. 2nd and Res. Challenge Prize at the Herts and Middlesex Show. Photo by Fall.

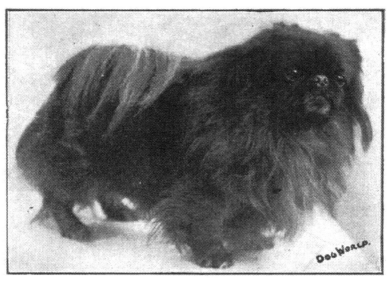

CA' TON WEN CHU, a beautiful dog belonging to **Mrs. MORREL,** of Ca' Ton Lodge. **WEN CHU** is siring splendid puppies. (Photo by Fall.

A group of Brood bitches all absolutely flat faced, belonging to **Mrs. R. MORREL** at Ca' Ton Lodge, Streatham.   (Photo by Fall.

Head Study of Mrs. **MORREL'S CA' TON WEN CHU.**

Yorkdale Kennels.

Mrs. LILLIAN LAWLEY-YORKE, 3540, WILTON AVENUE, CHICAGO, ILL., U.S.A.

Tsang of Rossmore, an exceptionally rich red with dark shadings, black muzzle, very short heavy boned forelegs, very sturdy and possesses the wonderful coat of the Goodwood strain, almost human in expression, lustrous large eyes, broad skull, a winner every time shown.

Sire of extremely flat faced puppies Imparts his fine points to his progeny.

Weight 10½ lbs.

Fee $25.00

TSANG OF ROSSMORE. A.K.C. 228501.

Perfect
Specimens
of
Pekingese
Puppies.

Yorkdale Kennels.

Mrs. LAWLEY-YORKE, 3540, WILTON AVENUE, CHICAGO, ILL.,
U.S.A.

IMPORTERS AND BREEDERS
OF PEKINGESE DOGS.

SHOW AND BREEDING STOCK FOR SALE
FROM THE MOST FASHIONABLE STRAINS.

Kennels Viewed by Appointment.

YORKDALE LEE.
A.K.C. 261215.

Yorkdale Lee is an unusually attractive "Sleeve" specimen of the Peke, being of that dark rich Chun Red, typical broad black mask, large luminous eyes, good skull, and coat, very flat face, forelegs short and well bowed, well defined waist line, truly a Lion Dog with all the characteristics of the perfect Peke. Proven sire of small flat faced puppies.

Weight 4½ lbs.   Fee $50.00

MAC NELLIE CHU-CHU.
By Faraline Yung Ching ex Mac Nellie Foo-Wong. **Fee 3 guineas.**

**MAC NELLIE
WEN-TI.**

A lovely First
Prize winner,
bred by
Mrs. Tritton.

**Fee
5 guineas.**

MAC NELLIE DEI-DEI.
By Nanking Wenti-Tu ex Normanhurst Lo-Wen.

Mrs. Tritton
with
**MAC NELLIE
SUN-TU:**

**Fee
3 guineas.**

RICHFLOWER

FOR BROOD BITCHES, INVALID DOGS, BAD DOERS, WEANING AND REARING PUPPIES.

No more puppies born dead or dying soon after birth, and no more weak-boned ricketty puppies.   To ensure strong, straight, healthy puppies being born the bitch's milk must be rich, pure and free from poisonous acids.   Rear your puppies to perfection by giving the dam **Richflower** daily for one month before and one month after whelping ; then commence giving it to the puppies, and continue until they are weaned.   It is very nutritious, easily digested and the most fastidious feeder will not refuse it.   Vets. recommend it, and most successful breeders and exhibitors use it extensively, and, considering what a short time it has been in the market, the heaps of testimonials prove what a boon and a blessing it is to all dog-breeders.   Please send for booklet.   When exhibiting, condition goes a great way towards winning.   Challenge certificate winner, Class 71, at Richmond, put down in such lovely condition by F. J. Matthews, Esq., had plenty of **Richflower**.   Puppies and dogs sell at a higher price and give greater satisfaction if clean, fat, healthy, strong, straight and sound.   Worms, lice, fleas and other troubles accumulate quickly in weak, delicate puppies and dogs.   Build up their strength by giving them **Richflower** and the rest will be easy.   Once used, always used, so please try it. **Richflower** sold in tins, **1s. 6d., 2s. 3d., 4s., 7s. 6d., 14s.,** post paid, direct from manufacturer only.

W. S. HUNT, Ottershaw, Chertsey.

ASHTON-MORE BUTTERFLY.

Mrs. GRIMWOOD'S PEKINGESE

At 104, Ashburton Avenue, Croydon, Surrey.

FOO-WONG OF KUANGTUNG

Son of Foo-Foo of Huron ex a daughter of Wee-Wong of Westbury
is a beautiful fawn with black mask and shadings, has won severa
times and is siring beautiful flat faced puppies.

His fee is 3 guineas.

CRINKLES OF EARLSFERRY.

By Ch. Chinky Chog ex Silver Queen of Earlsferry (Ch. Nanking Wenti). A well-known winner up to 1916. Born 1912, he is still in full vigour, and is probably the best as well as the best-known son of the late champion.

KO-KO OF EARLSFERRY.

By Remenham Biondello ex Mai Mao of Hackney Leven. A golden red, lion shape, squashed back face. Siring superb puppies. A lovely little dog. Weight 6 lbs.

The late **MAI MAO OF HACKNEY LEVEN,** with her sons by
Crinkles of Earlsferry.

CHOGGY CHINK OF EARLSFERRY.
By Crinkles ex Mai Mao of Hackney Leven. A wonderful little dog,
small, compact, immense bone, a perfect lion-shaped body, with
wonderful legs, and shortest possible face, golden red.

Rosemary Kennels.

37, THORNTON AVENUE,
STREATHAM HILL,
LONDON.

Cables *via* Western Union :
" ROSEMARY, LONDON."

WEST HARTFORD,
CONNECTICUT,
U.S.A.

Telegraphic Address :
" ROSEMARY, HARTFORD,
CONNECTICUT."

BREEDERS
AND IMPORTERS AND
EXPORTERS
OF
PEKINGESE,
ENGLISH TOY SPANIELS
POMERANIANS,
AND
GRIFFONS.

CH. ROSEMARY CALVERT.

ONE OF THE ROSEMARY PEKINGESE.

The Deodora Kennels.

MRS. THOMAS HOPKINS'

SHOW AND STUD DOG,

DEODORA H'SING,

AT CONNAMARA,
OXTED, SURREY.

TELEPHONE— NEW OXTED **155.**

DEODORA H'SING
(BORN FEB., 1916).

THE REMENHAM PEKINGESE.

The property of Mrs. VLASTO, at 92, Tulse Hill, S.W.2.

Ch. BRACKLEY BIONDINA.

By Sutherland Owen-Ten Tang ex Brackley Chinchilla.

Age 12 years.

THE REMENHAM PEKINGESE.

The property of Mrs. VLASTO, at 92, Tulse Hill, S.W.2.

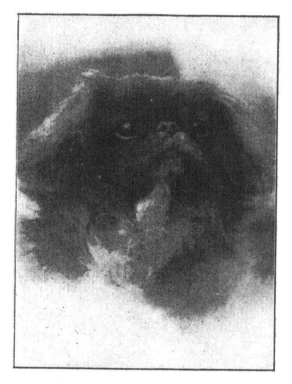

KU-SU OF REMENHAM.

By Ku-Erh of Remenham ex Sutherland Avenue Wen-ni.
At present unshown.

THE REMENHAM PEKINGESE.
The property of Mrs. VLASTO, at 92, Tulse Hill, S.W.2.

KU-SU OF REMENHAM.
By Ku-erh of Remenham, ex Sutherland Avenue Wen-ni.

PAT-SE OF REMENHAM.
By Sibton Tiny ex Go-hi of Remenham and his progeny, Maggie and Pat-se-tu.   Fee £10 10s.

THE REMENHAM PEKINGESE.

The property of Mrs. VLASTO, at 92, Tulse Hill, S.W.2.

Ch. KOTZINA OF REMENHAM.

By Ch. Kotzu of Burderop ex Ch. Brackley Biondina.

THE REMENHAM PEKINGESE.

The property of Mrs. VLASTO, at 92, Tulse Hill, S.W.2

REMENHAM BIONDELLO.

By Ch. Kotzu of Burderop ex Ch. Brackley Biondina.

Fee - £15 15s.

DEVATOL-A TABLETS.

The True Remedy for Impotence and Sterility in animals.

Before attempting to breed from any animal, owners should assure themselves that both sire and dam are in a fit state to perform the required function, and to obtain that fitness, a course of **Devatol-A** should be given before mating. As these tablets act only on the special centres, without affecting the heart, stomach, or bowels, there is no risk of unpleasant after effects, and a strong healthy litter is assured.

Per tube.
For small animals—yellow tablets **1/-**
For medium and heavy—grey ,, **1/6**
Of ten tablets, equalling 10 to 40 doses.

Send full particulars to—

CHAS. ZIMMERMANN & Co. (Chem.) Ltd.,
9-10, St. Mary-at-Hill, London, E.C.3.   ENTIRELY BRITISH FIRM.

Mrs. HASLOCKES' PEKINGESE AND JAPANESE,
At Kenley House, Kenley, Surrey.

A Typical Brace of Brood Bitches.
ADULTS AND PUPPIES OCCASIONALLY FOR SALE.

THE LOVELY LITTLE PEKINGESE

DAVINGTON BUNNY.

Born September 18th, 1908.

Colour, red with black mask.

Sire Orange Bay.   Dam Cleopatra of Eppingdale.

Owned by

Miss JENKINS, RECTORY COTTAGE, SYMONDSBURY, BRIDPORT.

176

Mrs. CROSS-BARRATT'S PEKINGESE,

At BON AIR, ST. SAVIOUR'S, JERSEY, C.I.

AT STUD.   ASHTON-MORE TARZAN.

A small fawn dog with wonderful bone and substance, very short legs, short back and short face. He carries an immense coat, and is siring very beautiful puppies.

Fee, 3 guineas.

BON AIR WOGS.

A very small silver fawn (under 4 lbs.), very short face (white blaze on forehead), fine eyes, good carriage and coat, short back.

Fee, 5 guineas at present.

Puppies occasionally for Sale.

NOTE.—Major-Gen. W. CROSS-BARRATT was the breeder of Ch. Chinky Chog.

177

Mrs. FOYER'S PEKINGESE, at The Warren, Stevenage.

WOO-CHU of The Warren.

Bred by Owner by **Ch. Lyncroft Chops** and **Siao-Nying** of The Warren.

Winner of many 1st and Special Prizes, Challenge Cups, etc.,
and sire of exceptionally good puppies.

Fee, 5 guineas.

DOA-WHA of The Warren.

By **Ashton-More Wen-Chu** and **Lu-Lu** of The Warren.

A fawn brindle Puppy, with remarkable head properties, practically
noseless, with firm underjaw, square face, immense eyes, also extra-
ordinarily heavy bone, and A1 legs.

Mrs. FOYER'S PEKINGESE, at The Warren, Stevenage.

**A basket full of Puppies by ASHTON-MORE WEN-CHU, and
ASHTON-MORE CHU-CHI.**

Their immense bone and wide flat faces are much in evidence.
Since the photo was taken they have won well at Championship Shows.

PAI-CHU of the Warren.
By **Ch. Choo Tai** of Moor Park and **Siao-Nying** of The Warren.

A beautiful bright mahogany red bitch, with truly wonderful coat.
plume and fringes.

Winner of many First Prizes.

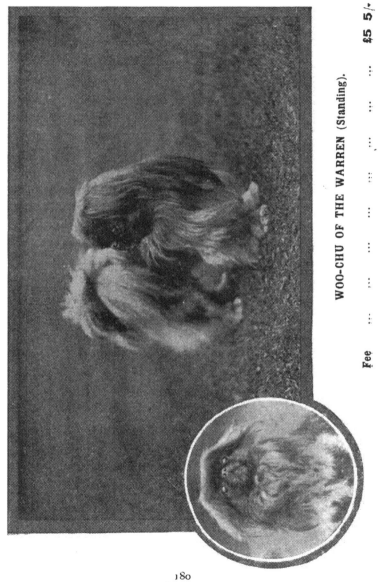

WOO-CHU OF THE WARREN (Standing).

Fee £5 5/-

THE TRAFFORD KENNELS,

At 553, STRETFORD ROAD, OLD TRAFFORD,
near MANCHESTER.

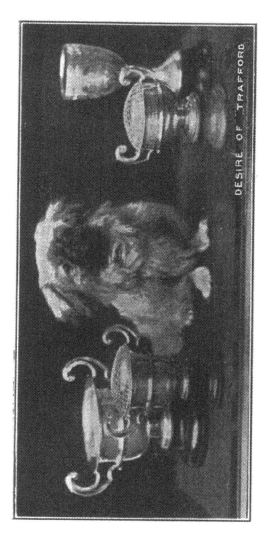

DESIRÉ OF TRAFFORD

AT STUD. By **Patsee of Kuen-Lun and Peggy of Trafford.**

Winner of 11 Firsts, 10 Seconds, 3 Thirds, and about 30 Special Prizes as a puppy. Under Mrs. Calley, Mrs. Raymond Mallock, Messrs. T. Marples, A. Marples, J. J. Holgate, T. Hooton, etc.

Fee ... ... **£4 4s.**

Also AT STUD. **BUBBLES OF TRAFFORD.**

An Extra Cobby Small Red Dog, with very big skull, and excellent eyes and bone. Chinatown bred on both sides. Fee ... **£4 4s.**

THE ASHCROFT PEKINGESE.

Mrs. Henry J. Weaver has selected " **Bon-ton of Ashcroft** " for illustration in this work, from many of her well-known winners. The life-like reproduction of his photograph shows his wonderful type to perfection. He is considered by more than one expert on the breed to be right at the top of his variety, and is probably one of, if not the best, ever sheltered in this world-renowned kennel.

His Fee is 20 Guineas to a limited number of approved bitches.

Apply Springfield House, Chalford Vale, near Stroud, Gloucester - shire.

BON-TON OF ASHCROFT.

Mrs. HUNTLEY-POCOCK'S PEKINGESE,

At 35, Manville Road, Tooting Common, S.W.17 (Balham Station).

MO-SHOS SUNNIE BOI.

Bred and Owned by Mrs. Huntley-Pocock.

Mo-Shos Sunni Boi is the winner of 2 First Prizes, Richmond 1920 ; 2 Firsts and 2 Specials, Hurlingham 1920, and 2 Seconds at Sandy Show 1920.

He is a red brindle with black mask and ear fringes, and is the sire of very lovely puppies.

Fee 7 Guineas.

THE PETERWOOD PEKINGESE, the property of
Mrs. WOOD-WEBSTER, 27, Beech Grove, Benton, Newcastle-on-Tyne.

AT STUD.

PHANTOM OF DENNISTOUN,

By ch. Phantom of Ashcroft. Already a winner of over 30 firsts, specials and cups for best Toy in show, and sire of numerous winners. Broad flat skull, perfectly flat face with very wide turned up muzzle, large dark prominent eyes, heavy bone, lion shaped body and wonderful wealth of coat, plume and feather.

Fee 3 guineas.

PEKOE OF PETERWOOD

is a perfect sleeve son of Phantom's, *ex* a ch. Chuerh of Alderbourne bitch. A replica of his sire, grand head, short face, large lustrous eyes, perfectly hung ears, extremely short, heavy, bowed legs and teeming with quality throughout.

Fee 2 guineas.

TONY OF PETERWOOD,

By that noted sire Mellerstain Yuen Yang, *ex* a bitch by ch. Howbury Ming. A gorgeous flame red, with black mask. Siring large litters of lovely puppies.

Fee 1 guinea.

Puppies and Adults usually for Sale.

Miss DE WINTON'S PEKINGESE,

At Abbots Lodge, nr. Gloucester.

PAY CHING CHU-TU and his Daughter **PAY CHING CHIN PAO.**
Weight 5¾lbs.   Fee **10 Guineas.**

Mrs. FRANKLIN BIERER'S PEKINGESE

At 5644, Beacon Street, Squirrel Hill, Pittsburgh Pa., U.S.A.,

Include the lovely imported dog

ASHTON-MORE SUDHOO

Winner every time shown and
said to be one of the most typical
Pekingese in the States to-day.

———

He has sired some wonderful puppies and is at stud to approved
bitches.

Mrs. TATE'S PEKINGESE at 55, Cantonments, Bareilly, India (Winter), St. Quentin-Naini-Tal (Summer).

KAULUNG ASHTON-MORE CHUM-CHU, Winner of 1st and Championships. The background is characteristic of an Indian Dog Show, the kennels being temporary mat. and bamboo structures. The scene is the 6th Lucknow Championship Show held by the United Provinces Club.

KAULUNG ASHTON-MORE CHUM CHU.

"Chummie" has won one Novice, one Limit, three Open and two Cups for best in Toy Breeds, one Special for best Pekingese in show and one Challenge Certificate. He has sired some of the finest puppies in India, including Kaulung Mo-li who caused a sensation at the Lucknow show, winning in four classes and was reserve for best puppy in the show. He weighs only 4½lbs. and should have a great future before him.

YAMA SING SING with some of her prizes won at Lahore Show, Christmas, 1919, owned by Mrs. RICHARDS, Mount Oswold, Murree, Punjab, India.

THE YOHYANG KENNELS.

DON-I OF YOHYANG

By Cho-Tan of Yohyang,

ex Wen-Shi of Yohyang.

A very beautiful Fawn Dog, with Black Mask.

— Exported to — Copenhagen, 1919.

CHO-TAN OF YOHYANG ..

By Ch. Chinky Chog

ex Be by Sutherland - oven - teu-tang.

Weight 8½lbs.

Fee - £5 5s.

All correspondence to :—

Mrs. ROLAND J. MACKAY,

22, Norfolk Road,

Seven Kings, Essex.

THE "VERITY" STUD DOGS

**PROPERTY OF QUEENIE VERITY-STEELE,
"STANTONS," LEWES, SUSSEX.**

PUPPIES AND BROOD BITCHES GENERALLY
FOR SALE ON APPLICATION.

Verity-Yu-Erh-Chu

Weight 8lbs.　　　Fee, 10 Guineas.

Also a wonderful " sleeve " red and white parti AT STUD—
" VERITY CUMSHAW "
ex " Bimbie of Witton " and " Kwai Kwai of Egham."

" VERITY HEI-PAO,"
Black grandson of " Ch. Phantom " and " Holywood Fan-Kwai."

Both absolutely noseless and lovely in type, coats and bearing.

THE "VERITY" STUD DOGS

**PROPERTY OF QUEENIE VERITY-STEELE,
"STANTONS," LEWES, SUSSEX.**

PUPPIES AND BROOD BITCHES GENERALLY
FOR SALE ON APPLICATION.

Weight 8lbs.   Fee, 10 Guineas.

Colour deep red, black mask (Bred by Lady Currie), son of " Ch. Chu
Erh Tu of Alderbourne " out of " Kinden Merrie " by " Wee Wong of
Westbury," and back to the Palace dog the late " Glanbrane Boxer,"
the ancestor of the late " Verity Buti Boi " and " Verity Bino."

THE "VERITY" STUD DOGS,

PROPERTY OF QUEENIE VERITY-STEELE,
"STANTONS," LEWES. SUSSEX.

Weight 8lbs.　　　　Fee, 10 Guineas.

FALL

"Verity Yu-Ert-Chu

The Bucklands Pekingese.

AT STUD.

CHU-TU OF BUCKLANDS.

The best Particolour Son of the late Ch. Chu-Tu of Alderbourne.

Fee 20 Guineas.

**The Property of Mrs. LEONARD HUBBARD,
The Bungalow, Datchet.**

Telephone WINDSOR **384.**

Red Fawn and Particolour Miniature Sons of above.

AT STUD.
Fees from 3 Guineas.

194

The Lovely Little

Blenheim Spaniel

PETER.

<small>OWNED BY</small>

Mrs. PENNINGTON,

2, Whitehall Court,

LONDON.

THE BISCUITS
FOR DOGS
"CITY MEAT.."

See each Biscuit is stamped thus ☞

Manufacturers and Proprietors:

WALKER, HARRISON & GARTHWAITES, LTD.,

PHŒNIX BISCUIT WORKS,
RATCLIFF CROSS, LONDON.

The First Bakers of Meat Biscuits for Dogs.

Championship Winners, regularly fed on " VISCAN."

Mrs. KEMP'S TOY SPANIELS AND PEKINGESE
At 33, Potter Street, Worksop.

BUBBLES (Tricolour Toy Spaniel).

Winner of 40 First Prizes, and sire of many very beautiful Puppies.
He is absolutely noseless with fine eyes, broad upturned muzzle,
massive head, and a wonderful coat.

GOULDESBOROUGH CARLO (Ruby).

Winner of 4 Firsts last time shown.

Fees ... 2 Guineas each.

Apply Mr. H. Taylor, 14, Main Road, Darnall, Sheffield.

Also AT STUD

High-class Pekingese including the well-known dogs :

DONOVAN OF GLEBELAND.   **Fee ... 3 Guineas.**
and
BARNEY OF BURTON ON DEE.   **Fee ... 3 Guineas.**

PEDMORE METEOR.

MERYL OF PEDMORE.

THE PEDMORE TOY SPANIELS,

the Property of Mrs. TRAVIS at Pedmore Grange, Stourbridge.

———

Mrs. Travis has been breeding Toy Spaniels for 20 years. During that time her principal object and study has been in "Breeding to type." Ch. Pedmore Vesta, Pedmore Meteor, and his progeny Ch. Lovedream of Pedmore, Ch. Melody of Pedmore, and Reverie, Rhapsody and Sonnet of Pedmore, etc., all bred by Mrs. Travis, prove what a success this study has been. **Fits and skin disease are unknown in these kennels, and Pedmore Meteor is the only one of its inmates which has ever had distemper.**

Mrs. CLEMENTS' TOY SPANIELS at 6, Kirby Road, Leicester.
Phone 4143.

A promising basketful of "Little Imps," bred by Mrs. Clements by
"Hentzau The Imp,"—Dam "The Brownie."
These Puppies are a wonderful combination of Ashton More, Advocate
and Pedmore blood.   Their dam is a sound Ruby brood sired by the
late beautiful Ashton-More Remus.

DILCOOSHA,
bred by
Mrs.   CLEMENTS.

A beautiful
Blenheim bitch, out
of Dame Martha,
and a worthy re-
presentative of her
Sire
Pedmore Meteor.

FREEMANS' RUSKS

(DIGESTIVE),

FOR SHY FEEDERS.

ASHTON-MORE LYNDA & TALISMAN.

SUIT ALL BREEDS AND AGES.

SPECIALLY BENEFICIAL TO TOY VARIETIES.

Are composed of the **very best and Purest Materials,** and are made upon a

SCIENTIFIC BASIS

for producing the best results and Preventing and Curing Indigestion, and

TENDING TO PREVENT AND CHECK WORMS.

They may be given to the **smallest and most delicate Dog,** and yet they are enjoyed by the **Largest and Strongest** Breeds. For Bitches in Whelp they are especially recommended.

In Boxes at 2/-, postage extra, **1/-,** or **3 Boxes for 7/-** post free.

Sold by all the big Stores. Any Chemist, Grocer, or Corn Merchant can obtain and supply them if he chooses to do so. If you cannot get them where you shop regularly, send to us direct.

FREEMANS' CAPSULED MEDICINES.

WORM, DISTEMPER, BLOOD, CONDITION, LIVER, COUGH

And every other necessary remedy, in sizes to suit all breeds and ages of dogs, **1/3, 2/9, 5/-** boxes. Send for full list.

These Gelatine Capsuled Medicines are without doubt the best and cleanest for Toy Dogs. They are highly recommended by Mrs. Raymond-Mallock, and are used by practically every well-known breeder and exhibitor of Toys.

FREEMANS', *Veterinary Chemists,*

CAUSEWAY MILLS, BLACKHEATH, BIRMINGHAM.

INTERNATIONAL CHAMPION—
CELAMO DAYDREAM.

Celamo Kennels,

19, SANFORD STREET, ROCHESTER, N.Y., U.S.A.

ENGLISH TOY SPANIELS EXCLUSIVELY.

Circulars Free.

PUPPIES
USUALLY FOR SALE

The Gleneesh Kennel of Toy Spaniels.

At 39, SACKVILLE GARDENS, ILFORD, ESSEX.

The Property of Mr. Lewis and Miss Violet Racine.

AT STUD.

RINALDO, Fee £1 1s.
(Prince Charles).

SAM PENTREATH, Fee £2 2s.
(King Charles).

COL SUNGOLD, Fee £1 1s.
(Prince Charles).

RINALDO.

ASHTON-MORE LITTLE MAN

KNIGHT'S KENNEL REGISTER & ACCOUNT BOOK.—Enables exhibitor to keep a detailed record of pedigree, stud, exhibiting account, and general expenses of the Kennel, and will be found of great utility. Size 10 by 8, bound in cloth; price **10/6.**

DOG SPECIAL ORDER REMOVAL BOOK.— 100 orders : price **3/6.**

DOG REMOVAL DEPOSIT AND RECEIPT BOOK.—100 receipts ; price **3/6.**

DOG REMOVAL ORDER CARDS.—250, price **9/6.**

DOG RING LEADER CARDS (with buttonhole).—3¾ by 3, numbered 1-100 ; price **4/6.**

DOG SHOW ARRIVAL AND DESPATCH SHEETS. Price **4/6** each.

DOG STUD FEE RECEIPT BOOK.—Price **3/6.**

DOG SERVICE CERTIFICATE BOOK.—Price **3/6.**

DOG PEDIGREE FORMS.—100, **6/-** ; 50, **3/6** : 25, **2/-**; 1 doz., **1/6.**

KNIGHT'S DUPLICATE MANIFOLD INTERLEAVED SHOW SECRETARIES' REGISTER, with duplicate index for exhibitors' names and addresses. Knight's improved Show Secretaries' Register saves time and money. Send schedules and ask for estimate.

ALL CLASSES OF SHOW PRINTING SUPPLIED.—Printing slips, Bench Number Cards, Roll Tickets, Illustrated Posters, **speciality:** Brooch Badges from **6/9** doz.

ARTISTIC DOG SHOW DIPLOMAS.—Printed in six colours and gold. Illustrated with eight splendid half-tone blocks of prize-winning dogs.

BACON & HUDSON, Show Printers, DERBY.

NO KENNELS SHOULD BE WITHOUT THEM.

GEO. WELCH'S

WORM CAPSULES

A Safe, Speedy and Certain Cure for all kinds of Worms.
The most convenient form for administering medicine to Dogs ever introduced.

No. 3 WORM CAPSULES
FOR TOY DOGS AND PUPPIES.

Sold in Boxes, 1/3, 2/6 and 5/-, Post Free.   Cash with Order.

Why use .... GEO. WELCH'S WORM CAPSULES ?	BECAUSE they are a Certain Cure. BECAUSE they are a perfectly Safe Remedy. BECAUSE they are Easily Administered. BECAUSE they are used in the best Kennels in the Kingdom. BECAUSE they are Recommended by Members of the Royal College of Veterinary Surgeons. BECAUSE they have stood the test for 20 years.

Sole Maker : **E. L. P. PARKER, Chemist,**
CASTLE DONINGTON, near Derby.

Miss KATHLEEN OATWAY'S

KING CHARLES SPANIEL,
LITTLE BILLY,

At 122, Claude Road, Roath,

CARDIFF.

LITTLE BILLY.

A beautiful specimen of his variety is LITTLE BILLY. He is the progeny of well-known Toy Spaniels, having Little Tim as sire, and is a grandson of the Ruby, Little Ticker,

        Ch. "Royal Rip,"

        Ch. "Merry Duke,"

        Ch. "Harford Jumbo," and many others.

Best of Breeds figure in his Pedigree.

COPPERGOLD.

Grandson of the two famous Rubys, Ch. Encore and Rough Diamond.

Fee, 3 Guineas.

PUPPIES OCCASION-ALLY FOR SALE.

MELITA KENNELS (REG.)

ANNA R. JUDD, Owner.

914, W. CROCKETT STREET, SEATTLE, WASHINGTON.

Telephone Queen Anne 399.

WESTERN HOME OF THE PURE MALTESE TERRIERS.

Stars of the Melita Kennels are : Normacot Camille, Normacot White King, Studebaker Namur, owned by these Kennels, Melita Sally, Melita Lady Meneris, Queen of Melita, Ch. Prince Melita and International Champion Melita Cupid, Champion and International Winner Melita Snow Dream. None of the above are for Sale.

International Ch. MELITA CUPID.

Champion and International Winner MELITA SNOW DREAM, Weight 3½lbs. Holds highest record in America, having taken **Best in Show, all Breeds,** once, and twice **Reserve to Best in Show,** and once **Third Best in Show, all Breeds.** With her Brother International Champion MELITA CUPID, three times **Best Brace in Show, all Breeds,** and at New York City, at Westminster Show, twice **Best Maltese Brace. Value $5,000.**

THE BEVERLAC KENNELS OF JAPANESE AND PEKINGESE.

Owned by Mrs. B. Cooper.

At 8, Beech Grove, Beverley Road, Hull.

A litter of promising puppies bred by Mrs. COOPER.

PRIZE DOGS AT STUD AND PUPPIES ALWAYS FOR SALE.

Mrs. Cooper will be pleased to show her dogs at any time by appointment.

Madam OSTERVENE'S JAPANESE, at 11, Church Road, St. Leonards-on-Sea.

Madam Ostervene with some of her Noted Winners.

WEE WANA, 3½lbs., has won well wherever shown and was sold for a big sum.

LITTLE NICHETTE, 4lbs. (in Madam Ostervene's lap), won 1st Open Bitches, at Richmond.

MINOR, 5lbs., also won well at Richmond.

The other two dogs, **LORNIE** and **TWEENY,** have not yet been shown.

All are home bred and by Madam Ostervene's own stud dogs and they are all house pets.

Some GRIFFONS BRUXELLOIS in Mrs. G. J. MORGAN'S Coptharrow Kennels, Restharrow, Godalming.

COPTHARROW NIEDA

By Ch. Copthorne Pick o' the Pack.

COPTHORNE SOPHIA

A noted Brood Bitch.

PUPPIES AND ADULTS USUALLY FOR SALE.

Some GRIFFONS BRUXELLOIS in Mrs. G. J. MORGAN'S Coptharrow Kennels, Restharrow, Godalming.

COPTHORNE TROUBADOUR

Winner of Challenge Certificate first time shown.

The sire of lovely Puppies, including Pax of St. Margaret's, who also won Challenge Certificate first time shown.

Fee £5 5s.

THE BRABARICON, KIM OF COPTHARROW

A "War Baby," siring certain winners.

Fee £5 5s.

Ch. Copthorne Firebrand, Ch. Copthorne Pick o' the Pack, and six other noted Dogs at Stud. Fees £3 3s. to £8 8s.

GRIFFON BRUXELLOIS DOG

BRED BY

Miss CURTIS,

ENTRY HILL HOUSE, BATH.

Phone No. : Bath 779.

JENY.

THE WONDERFUL " CHINATOWN " DOGS.

CHAMPION PUN CHIN OF CHINATOWN.

Brilliant Winning Record.   Fee 8 Guineas.

These Dogs are the finest Stud Dogs ever benched ; they are all magnificent Show Dogs, perfect in type.

Mr. and Mrs. WEIL, Dock House, Lytham, Lancashire.

THE WONDERFUL " CHINATOWN " DOGS.

T'SAN PAM OF CHINATOWN.
Reserve Champion and Big Winner.   Fee 6 Guineas.

LI OF CHINATOWN.
Big winner and incomparable sire of winning progeny. ˙Fee 4 Guineas.

Miss VIOLET K. BLAIKLOCK

Photographs, Children and Dogs in their own homes. Terms from
2 Guineas a Dozen; Travelling Expenses extra.

— 18, ELSWORTHY ROAD, LONDON, N.W. 3. —

Telephone : Hampstead **4884.**

Mrs. PEARL ZELLEN'S PEKINGESE

At Tammarache Hall, Winchester, Wisconsin, U.S.A.

McINTYRE HEATH OF TAMMARACHE HALL.

One of the Tammarache Hall stud dogs reserved for use in these kennels. He is not at public stud. Mrs. Zellen has some half dozen beautiful brood bitches also, they live amidst ideal surroundings at her charming country home which is located in the Northern Woods of Wisconsin. Here they romp about and play to their heart's content and get into condition for the Winter Shows. Tammarache Hall has 46 acres of lake frontage. The buildings are all up to date, with dormitories and sun parlours (made of cedar logs and grass), where the little pets play on rainy days. The Tammarache Pekes all have absolutely flat faces, as Mrs. Zellen cannot tolerate a "nose."

Mrs. MARIE MAY'S PEKINGESE,
At 72, Huron Road, Tooting Common, London.

SU-TI OF HURON.

A glorious black bitch, absolutely noseless, with great ear fringes, a perfect Peke and one of the soundest blacks ever seen.

BEETLE OF HURON.

A lovely little black and tan, grandson of Foo - Foo of Huron, out of a litter sister to Ch. Yen Foo of Huron. Weight 4½lbs. He is absolutely perfect

Photos reproduced by special permission of *The Dog World*

HEAD STUDY OF FOO-FOO OF HURON.
Sire of Champion Yen-Fuh of Huron and many other winners.

LI-CHING OF HURON.
A son of Foo-Foo.   Red sable with a true Peke front, flat face,
glorious coat and good shaped body.

Photos reproduced by special permission of *The Dog World.*

Prize Winning **Toy Spaniel Puppies** owned and bred by the Authoress of this book.

Mrs. Raymond-Mallock writes :—

" I am very pleased to recommend your **GROATS** as a food for Puppies and nursing Mothers. I use it extensively in my kennels."

ROBINSON'S GROATS,

THE BEST FOOD FOR PRIZE AND PEDIGREE DOGS, AND ALL KINDS OF TOY AND FANCY BREEDS.

A cheaper form of **Robinson's Groats** is now prepared under the name of **Robinson's " Animal " Groats,** and is sold in 14lb. bags, obtainable through any Corn Dealer or Stores.

KEEN, ROBINSON& CO., Ltd., LONDON.

Mrs. ARTHUR BAKER'S PEKINGESE,

At MOOREND,

CHARLTON KINGS, CHELTENHAM.

CH. ZAN-SE.

Whelped April 1st, 1914.   Red with black mask.

Sire, Sibton Tiny.   Dam, Holywood Woo-Woo.

222

FLASHAWAY OF DARA.

Bred by Owner. A very beautiful youngster, who is the most brilliant Orange Pom ever shown, a pure orange without a single black hair. Weight 3½lbs. He is as near perfection as any Pom has been, with a marvellously short back, immense coat, and an exquisite head, perfectly chiselled and very fine. He is a big winner at the leading shows, and many big offers have been refused for him.

FIRELIGHT OF DARA.

Bred by Owner. One of the best known Poms of his day, and famous all the world over as the sire of noted winners.

224

Mrs. ELLA WITHERS,

BREEDER OF FIRST CLASS STOCK,

HAS ALWAYS FOR SALE—

BROOD BITCHES, YOUNG DOGS AND GOOD PUPPIES,

by AH SIN OF NOKE,

AT REASONABLE PRICES.

CAN BE SEEN ANY TIME BY APPOINTMENT.

Telephone :
1871 RICHMOND.

36, *ELM ROAD*,
EAST SHEEN,
SURREY.

RACKHAM'S DOG MEDICINES

HAVE BEEN USED IN THE FOREMOST KENNELS OVER 70 YEARS.

—RACKHAM'S JAPANESE WORM POWDERS.

A tasteless and most certain remedy. " One dose sufficient."
They are also a splendid alternative medicine for all dogs.
Price 7½d., 1/3, 2/9, 5/-, 10/-, 20/-; free 2d. extra.

—RACKHAM'S DISTEMPER BALLS.

The only cure for Distemper known, no matter at what stage.
Have been used in the principal kennels for 50 years.
Price 1/3, 2/9, 5/-, 10/-, 20/-; free 2d. extra.

—RACKHAM'S KATALEPRA.

Cures Red Mange, Eczema, and all Skin Diseases.
Price 1/3, 2/9, 5/-, 10/-, 20/-; free 4d. extra.

Send for a free Booklet on Dog Ailments to
RACKHAM & CO., 25, Week Street, Maidstone.

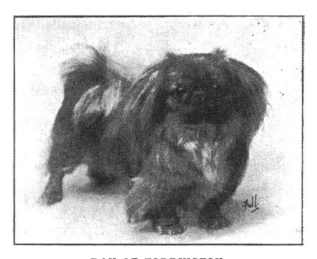

DAN OF TODDINGTON.
Sire, Palace Chang Yao Cheng ex Hua of Toddington.
Weight 8½lbs.   Winner of many prizes.

DAN OF TODDINGTON.
Stud Fee at present, 5 guineas.

Mrs. HUGH ANDREWS' PEKINGESE

At Toddington Manor, Winchcombe, Gloucestershire.

TONI HSIN OF TODDINGTON

By Chun-Chang of Alderbourne ex Hua of Toddington.

Red with black mask and shadings.   Weight 7lbs.

Stud fee, **10** Guineas.

Winner of two firsts, three seconds and one third, Unwin Puppy
Cup for best puppy bred by a member of Cheltenham and Gloucester
Canine Society, Cheltenham, 1916.   During 1920 he has won four
firsts, five seconds and Douglas Murray Cup at L.K.A., P.P.D.A.,
Herts and Middlesex, Cheltenham and Guildford Shows.

Miss DUFFIELD JONES' PEKINGESE, Melville Lodge, BOGNOR.

" MI BEETLE."

Sire—Ch. Broadoak Beetle.

Dam—Grand-daughter of Ch. Chu'erh of Alderbourne.

Red, black mask, short broad face, large dark eyes, heavy bone, very low to ground. beautiful coat and feathering.

FEE £3 3s.

Puppies usually for sale.

THE "LADYCROSS" KENNEL OF PEKINGESE.

This is a select but small kennel, whose aim is to breed the best. The dogs live almost entirely out of doors, and everything is done to make them as healthy and happy as possible. Nothing of a weedy or lap-dog description is kept. There are two Stud-dogs ; The Chiki-Idol of Ladycross, a perfect sleeve red and white parti, and Ladycross Choo-Chog, a fawn with black mask and shadings. Both these dogs are small typical Chinamen, and proud sires. Puppies occasionally for sale. *Full particulars from*

Miss IRIS ROPER, Ladycross, Seaford. 'Phone 52 Seaford.

THE WHIPPENDELL PEKINGESE.

WHIPPENDELL ALAADIN.

By Lamphey Quizy ex Whippendell Shola.

Bred and owned by Miss BRUNKER, Whippendell House, King's Langley.

A brilliant red dog with jet black mask. Absolutely noseless, with wonderful flat broad face and strong jaw, massive head, good featherings, and excellent shape and mover. Winner of many prizes at the principal Championship Shows.

Fee 7 Guineas.

THE PEKECLAN KENNELS.

**Property of Madame MARIE ANTIONETTE SCHEIBE, at " Clarendon,"
28, Elliot Road, Thornton Heath, Surrey.**

NANKING WU.

One of the noted Pekeclan Stud Dogs, son of Champion Nanking
Wenti ex Champion Nanking Tsung Ming, red and white parti-colour,
noseless, with wonderful head, legs and bone.

This Kennel is noted for its type and quality.

Puppies and Adults can always be purchased for Show and
Pets at reasonable prices, and seen at any time.

*PEKECLAN PUPPY FOOD, manufactured by Madame Scheibe
has won great reputation as a valuable asset in rearing Puppies.*

CHAMPION OUEN-CHU-T'SAN OF THORPE,

At Six Months old.

By T'san Pam of Chinatown ex Ashton More Dee Dee.

Bred by Mrs. ETHRINGTON.

Winner, at fifteen months old, of seven Challenge Certificates, two Reserves for the Challenge Certificate, 1st and Best Pekingese at the L.K.A. Members' Show, and 1st and Best Bitch at the P.P.D.A. Show.

———

The property of Mrs. SLINGSBY, Tickton Hall, Beverley, East Yorks.

ASHTON-MORE PINKEE.

ELASTENE

(REGISTERED TRADE MARK),

THE POPULAR PRE-WAR

—— BEDDING ——

IS STILL THE **BEST** FOR

SPORTING,

TOY AND

OTHER DOGS.

233

245

Miss MADELINE DINGLEY'S PEKINGESE,
At 1151, WASHINGTON STREET, SO. BRAINTREE, MASS., U.S.A.

MEDOR CHING-SU.

Miss AMY MILLER'S PEKINGESE,
At ST. THOMAS, EAST COWES, I.W.

AT STUD—THE BEAUTIFUL LITTLE DOG—

ST. THOMAS HO.

A worthy son of Sutherland Avenue Ho. He has a wonderful head, very good front, splendid body, and a profuse coat.

Winner of two first prizes, special for best dog first time shown, and three seconds next time shown.

He is the sire of really good puppies.

Fee   ...   ...   £5   5   0.

PUPPIES AND ADULTS OCCASIONALLY FOR SALE.

Mrs. LE BERT'S PEKINGESE,

At Newlands, Woodland Road, W., Colwyn Bay.

A CHARMING GROUP OF MRS. LE BERT'S FAVOURITES.

CHARMETTE.—A lovely little parti-coloured bitch (deep red and white).

COWSLIP.—Smart red and white parti-coloured dog, litter brother to Butterfly, and sire of lovely puppies.

BARNEY O'HEA.—A beautiful sable with immense coat.

BUTTERFLY.—A lovely Chun red dog with black mask, Ch. Chinky Chog, Ch. Chuerh of Alderbourne and Ch. Chin-Lu strains. Siring exquisite puppies. Fee, **3** guineas.

THE NEWNHAM PEKINGESE

The property of Mrs. HERBERT COWELL, at 46, Brunswick Square,

Hove.

AT STUD.

CHU OF NEWNHAM.

By Nanking Wen-Chu ex Betty II. Clear fawn.
Weight 8½lbs.

Fee - - **5 guineas.**

HUNG-TI OF NEWNHAM

By Caesar of Winkfield. Weight 9lbs. Bright red
and white particolour.

Fee - - **5 guineas.**

KIN-EE OF NEWNHAM.

Bright red. Weight 7lbs.

Fee - - **5 guineas.**

TO-NI OF NEWNHAM.

By Faraline Yung Ching. Dark red, black mask.
Weight 5lbs.

Fee - - **5 guineas.**

THE NEWNHAM PEKINGESE

The property of Mrs. HERBERT COWELL, at 46, Brunswick Square,

Hove.

CH. YEN CHU OF NEWNHAM

Bred by Mrs. COWELL.

By Ch. Chuerh of Alderbourne ex Glenbrane Qui-Qui.

NOTICE.—It is with deep regret we announce the death of this grand old dog, which occurred after the above photo had been reproduced.

Miss PHELIPS' PEKINGESE, at 10, Beach Road, Littlehampton.

ASHTON-MORE SUET KOU (SNOWBALL).

By Ashton-More Wen-Chu ex Ashton-More Fan-Tan. A pure white puppy with immense dark eyes and a jet black nose. This is a specimen of the lovely puppies Miss Phelips occasionally has for disposal.

Mrs. P. SHRUBB'S PEKINGESE,
At Trelawney, 94, Pretoria Road, Thrale Road, Streatham, S.W.16.

KIN CHAU WONG (Wee Wong of Westbury ex Portelet Kin Chau, bitch), red, with marvellous head, black face, very short bowed legs, heavy bone, short cobby body and massive coat. He is one of Wee Wong's last sons. Sires miniatures in every litter.

TANGERINE KING (Tiny Nin Chou of Dunsmore ex bitch by Nanking Wen-Chu). Bright orange, massive head, short cobby body, sire of beautiful bright red puppies, very strong and healthy.

YOUNG CHING, Jun. (Faraline Young Ching ex Foo Mi of Huron bitch), red, miniature black flat face, very showy little dog, weight 5lbs. Fee to either, **£2 2s.**

Only the very highest class Bitches bred from in this Kennel.

Puppies usually for sale.

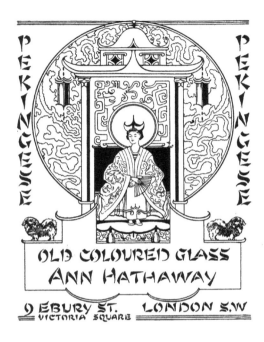

PEKINGESE PEKINGESE

OLD COLOURED GLASS
ANN HATHAWAY
9 EBURY ST.   LONDON S.W.
VICTORIA SQUARE

ANN   HATHAWAY
HAS THE FINEST
COLLECTION
OF OLD
COLOURED GLASS
IN LONDON.

—o—

COLLECTORS ARE
INVITED
TO INSPECT.

Also THE LO-YANG PEKINGESE.

AT STUD.

THE PALACE BRED DOGS.

FEE - 5 Guineas each.

VERITY CHEN-YO. Grandson of CH. PHANTOM OF ASHCROFT and the imported PRINCESS SING OF BRAYWICK. Grey brindle, black faced.

LO-YANG CHIA CHU. Son of VERITY TU'ERH CHU by CH. CHU'ERH TU. Flat faced, parti-colour.

LO-YANG CHOW FONG. Brilliant red, black mask, son of VERITY TU'ERH CHU ex the well-known bitch VERITY JOSETTE. (Will be at Public Stud in March, 1921).

PUPPIES AND ADULTS FOR SALE.

Ch. ANDERSON MANOR JIRO.

The column by his side bears his name in Japanese.

He won 1st prize also Best in Show at Tokio previous to his coming to England

Ch. ANDERSON MANOR TUKI.

Home bred in her own little genuine Chippendale bedstead with wheatear posts and original old hangings.

Mrs. GORDON GREATRIX'S JAPANESE,
At Ixworth Abbey, Bury St. Edmunds.

A CHARMING GROUP OF IMPORTED JAPS.

Ch. ANDERSON MANOR JIMAYO.

Ch. ANDERSON MANOR JAKURO.

Ch. ANDERSON MANOR HOKUSAI.

Ch. ANDERSON MANOR CHIGI.

Ch. ANDERSON MANOR OKO,
A very beautiful imported Bitch (Weight 3lbs.)

Mrs. HENRY FRASER'S PEKINGESE,
At Brackendene, Barnes Common, S.W.

Champion FARALINE WEN TZU.

Beautiful fawn daughter of Ch. Faraline Tzu Chu and Ch. Nanking
Wen Ti. Bred by Mrs. Fraser, and litter sister to Ch. Faraline
She Mei Tzu.

Head Study of Champion FARALINE WEN TZU.

Mrs. HENRY FRASER'S PEKINGESE,
At Brackendene, Barnes Common, S.W.

Champion FARALINE TZU CHU.
Beautiful red bitch, most perfect type.   Bred by Mrs. Fraser.

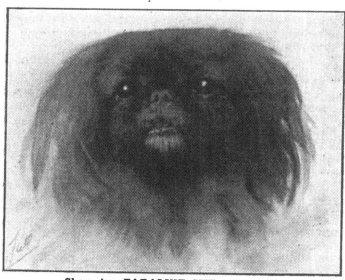

Champion FARALINE SHE MEI TZU.
Lovely red daughter of Ch. Faraline Tzu and Ch. Nanking Wen Ti.
Bred by Mrs. Fraser.

Mrs. BORLEY'S PEKINGESE,
At The Cedars, Esher, Surrey. Phone Esher 176.

REMENHAM BENI.
PEDIGREE :

Sire—	Sutherland Ouen Teu Tang	⎰ Manchu Tao Tai ⎱ Manchu Wei Wei	⎰ Ch. Goodwood Chun. ⎱ Ch. Gia Gia. ⎰ Ch. Manchu Cheng 'Tu ⎱ Ch. Palace Shi.
Dam—	Wiggy Woggy	⎰ Ch. Chinky Chog ⎱ Tufnell Sister Mary	⎰ Jabber Wock. ⎱ Howdie. ⎰ Broadoak Billy. ⎱ Oudema.

Sire of numerous winners, including " FAI OF ALDERBOURNE,"
who won Reserve Championship at Cruft's at the age of 8 months.
He has beaten Ch. Swinley Li Lien four times out of six.

SHOW WINS.   WEIGHT 9lbs.
1914.
A grandly coated red sable dog.

At the Joint Show, Westminster (under Miss Keith Wright), he won
2nd Puppy, 3rd Novice, 3rd Graduate.   At the L.K.A. Open
Show, 2nd Junior in a class of 16.

At the P.P.D.A. (under Mrs. Seely Clarke), 2nd Puppy in a class of 18,
and Kingham Trophy for Best Puppy bred by Exhibitor.

At the Pekingese Club (under Major Becher), 2nd Novice in a class
of 20.

At Richmond (under Mr. Weil), 2nd Novice in a class of 17, 2nd
Graduate in a class of 16.

At Bexhill (under Mrs. Becher), 1st Novice, 2nd Junior, 2nd Graduate
and 2nd Special Limit.

At People's Palace (under Mrs. Kennedy), 1st Graduate, 1st Special
Limit and 2nd Limit.

1915.
At Cruft's (under Mrs. Weaver), 2nd Limit, 3rd Open, Ebury Cup and
Special.

1916.
At L. and P.P.C. (under Mr. Astley), 1st Limit and 2nd Open.
At People's Palace (under Mrs. Slingsby), 1st Limit.

WILSON'S
IMPROVED CAPSULES

FOR THE RAPID EXTERMINATION AND CURE OF WORMS IN PEKES & TOY DOGS.

Sold in Two Strengths in boxes at 2/6 and 5/- Post Free.
Cash with order.

CH. ASHTON DEFENDER.

THE ABSOLUTE STANDARD OF WORM MEDICINES.

RALPH WILSON,
45, Main Street, Uddingston, Lanarkshire, Scotland.

AMERICAN AND CANADIAN AGENCY :
Mrs. G. E. TAYLOR, The Henry Clay Hotel, Detroit, Mich.

THE HOMEFIELD PEKINGESE.

At Stud: "CHENGTU of HOMEFIELD"

(A Winner every time shown).

Bright red, black mask, flat strong face, gorgeous coat, big bone, beautifully balanced throughout. Siring winners. The latest success of his progeny is "YOUNG SHI OF HOMEFIELD," a full Canadian Champion at 11 months old. Won through all her classes, Toronto, and cups for best Peke; the Canadian National Show, from Puppy to open, winning club cups and medals; Ottawa Show ditto; the Toy Dog Show of Canada ditto, under different judges each time, and still undefeated.

Fee and Particulars on application to

Mrs. KAY, HOMEFIELD, WHITEFIELD, LANCASHIRE.

Miss LOUISE HOCKEY'S PEKINGESE AND POMERANIANS
At 48, Hartington Street, Derby.

MISS HOCKEY owns a small but select kennel of PEKINGESE AND POMERANIANS, "HALS MING" and "YUE LAOU" being her two Peke stud dogs. "Hals Ming" is a lovely rich coloured red sable, with flat black mask, a perfect front and huge coat and plume. His sire was Ch. Howbury Ming, his dam, "Beda," by "Olo Peen of Toddington," "Beda" was dam of "Portelet Kin Chaw" and other winners.

,, YUE LAOU" is a lovely small red dog, a grandson of the late "Kwai Kwai of Egham" and "Ashton-More Ming." Miss Hockey has some lovely puppies by these dogs, and has sold some for big prices.

Another brood bitch is the Red Sable "BROWNIE LING" (reg.), who owns as grandsires the famous Ch. Chuerh of Alderbourne, and Ch. Chinky Chog.

Miss Hockey has several Poms, her old favourite, "BRIGHT GOLD," by Bright Banshee, still looking well and lively, although 9 next birthday; "Little Wolf," a most charming tiny Sable puppy, looks like doing well when shown. Nearly five months' old and under 3lbs. weight, his style, tail carriage and action are perfect. His shape, tone and head are all that can be desired and his tiny ears are nearly hidden by his coat. He is by Little Candidate, out of Wendy by Ch. Mars.

A good brood bitch, has puppies by a son of Ch. Mars, and another little orange bitch by "Bright Gold" complete the kennel. All are in perfect health and condition.

STOCK USUALLY FOR SALE.

NAME TALLIES.

ASHTON-MORE CHU-WEI.

Quong Foy of Foo Choo.
SON OF THE LATE CH. BROADOAK BEETLE.

Jet black, rich tan feathering, perfect front, massive bone, low to ground.

Siring large litters of small puppies.

Weight 9lb.

Verity Lo Foo.
6½lbs.   SIRE, THE LATE VERITY BUTI BOI.

Chun-red, with black mask, absoultely noseless, smashed-in face, glorious eyes, good bone and carriage.

Siring lovely puppies.

Fee - 3 Guineas.

Mrs. BLADEN JONES, 84, Francis Street, Leeds.
Bitches met at Leeds.

Mrs. HARE'S PEKINGESE,

At Gilbury, Exbury, Hants.

GILBURY BING-BOY.

A red and white beautifully marked Particolour.

By Ch. Chuty of Alderbourne ex Verity Lyndah.

Born July 12th, 1916.

Weight 7½lbs.

Fee - - - 2 Guineas.

Mrs. HAROLD TAYLOR'S PEKINGESE,

At Prospect House, Lostock, near Bolton.

BOLTONIA CHONG.

By SIBTON TINY ex a daughter of WEN OF EGHAM.

He is a light red, with huge dark perfect eyes, tail carried always perfectly, absolutely fearless. His nose is placed right up between the eyes, and is embedded in wrinkles. He has good bone, well bowed legs, and is low to ground. In fact a grand Peke all over. Weight 9¾ lbs.

FEE - 10 Guineas.

Dogs and Bitches Sold from this Kennel since 1919 have won 10 Championships in England and dozens of Prizes.

Mrs. HAROLD TAYLOR'S PEKINGESE,

At Prospect House, Lostock, Near Bolton.

RODDY OF HARTLEBURY.

A magnificent red, with large dark eyes. Flat well-wrinkled face, very low to ground. Tremendous bone. Good coat and tail carriage. Winner of innumerable prizes, and many times Special for Best in Show.

His puppies are very good, and have won many prizes. His litter at Altringham won First in a big Class.

He is a grandson of Kwai-Kwai of Egham, and Sutherland Ouen Teu Tang.

FEE (at present) - 4 Guineas.

All the brood bitches in this kennel are of the finest quality, with flat faces, good bone, and bowed legs.

HAVE YOU TRIED
—— THE. NEW ——

MOLASSINE

Dog and Puppy Biscuits

—— IF NOT, WRITE FOR FULL ——
PARTICULARS & SAMPLE TO-DAY.

These Biscuits are absolutely unique. They are equal in appearance and quality to the best on the market, AND IN ADDITION have digestive and antiseptic properties found in no others.

They eradicate worms and keep all dogs and puppies in the pink of condition.

BY APPOINTMENT.

MANUFACTURED ONLY BY

THE MOLASSINE CO., LTD., GREENWICH, LONDON

(City Office : 28, MARK LANE, E.C.)

THE PORTLET PEKINGESE

CHAMPION LYNCROFT CHOPS AND CHU CHIN CHOW OF LYNCROFT.

The Property of Mr. H. F. Laughton, 5, St. James's Terrace, Regent's Park, N.W.
Phone : Hampstead 3696.

Photo : Fall.]   **Ch. Lyncroft Chops and Chu Chin Chow of Lyncroft.**   [*Baker St., W.*

The world-famous champion, Lyncroft Chops, is known to fanciers in both hemispheres.   What a career this dog would have had but for the world's war tragedy, which lost him five of the best years of his life !   Yet so great is his excellence that he has scored no less than seven championships.

He has a perfect head, with lovely eyes and expression, a deep square muzzle and enormous flat skull.   In body he is absolutely perfect, such depth throughout, with a very slim waist, his mane is lion-like, and his stern comes right over to the back of his skull.   He is bred " in the purple," so it can be easily understood that as a sire this most typical champion has done remarkable service to the breed. Amongst his progeny may specially be enumerated Si-Li, champion dog, Brussels ; Chop Sticks, champion bitch, Australia ; Sunden Sing Tau, reserve champion dog, Richmond ; Lyncroft Ah Ling, Lyncroft Ah Sam, Woo Choo of the Warren, Chips of Elsworthy, Ou Fus, Ko Foo Kum and Sai Kinchau of Roadside, Quimbo of Earlsferry, Chops Sun of Elvaston, Ashton More Chutzi, Gresham Toi, Ch. Viola Ashcroft America, best dog in show, Atlantic City.   One of the greatest sights for owners of stud dogs to see was the remarkable gathering of the excellent sons and daughters of Ch. L. Chops at the recent show of Pekingese at Hurlingham for the stud dog prize.   It perhaps has never been equalled.   His stud fee is £10 10s.

Chu Chin Chow of Lyncroft is but eighteen months old, therefore has plenty of time ahead, for Pekes, like wine, improve with age. Yet he has already started on a convincing career against the best specimens.   He is an all-red son of Ch. Lyncroft Chops and grandson of Mougal of Yaou Tsing.   The latter dog, Major Cox, R.A., M.C., imported from the Imperial Palace, and he is guaranteed pure Palace-bred.   Chu Chin Chow's blood is now invaluable, as there can be no more stock from the same source on account of the Revolution.   He is a grand-boned dog, with first-rate body and movement, as sound as a hound, with massive skull, true Peke coat and well featured.   He is now placed at stud, and his fee for a time will be £3 3s.

THE PRIZE-WINNING SCHIPPERKE—

Champion LEIGH TOMMY ATKINS.
K.C.S.B., 1604, R.   Born May 25th, 1910.

AT STUD.

"LEIGH TOMMY ATKINS" excels in coat, body, feet and legs,
Foxey head, small ears and dark eye.

———

WON FIVE CHAMPIONSHIPS.

MANCHESTER—May, 1915. Judge : Mr. J. T. Greenhalgh.
RICHMOND—July, 1915. Judge : Mrs. G. H. Killick.
CRUFTS—1916. Judge : Mr. Bremet.
RANELAGH—L.K.A., 1916. Judge : Dr. C. D. Freeman.
RANELAGH—L.K.A., May, 1920. Judge : Mrs. Grace.

DOG PORTRAITS.

MISS MAUD MOLYNEUX,
47, PORTLAND ROAD,
HOVE, . . SUSSEX.

ANIMAL PORTRAIT PAINTER,

Desires to inform owners of favourite dogs that she undertakes Commissions for Painting Full-length or Head Portraits of Dogs.

She has executed numerous paintings for persons of eminence and well-known dog lovers, which have met with general approval.

She pays great attention to the details of her paintings, and has been particularly successful with Out-door Pictures in Gardens and other Landscape surroundings.

HER TERMS ARE

FULL-LENGTH PORTRAITS £5 5s.
HEADS - from £2 2s. to £3 3s.

MRS. GENT'S VARIETY KENNELS OF PEKINGESE, JAPANESE GRIFFONS AND POMERANIANS,

At Warrenhurst, Barton-on-Sea, New Milton, Hants.

Dogs from these kennels have gone all over the world, including America, Holland, Buenos Ayres, South Africa, Italy, Sweden, France, &c. They always give satisfaction, and may be relied upon as being really typical specimens of the best blood procurable.

Stock for Sale at Moderate Prices.

"HENTROSE" SKIN LOTION.

MANGE.—Wash the affected animal, and when dry gently rub the lotion on the skin (preferably with an old tooth brush) on five consecutive days—then wash. In most cases this will have effected a cure. When cured, the top skin will gradually peel off, causing no inconvenience to the patient.

ECZEMA, BLOTCH, RASH, AND PIMPLES.—Treatment as for Mange, but three consecutive dressings should be sufficient. Care should be taken to apply the lotion around as well as on to the affected parts.

To grow coat, apply where luxuriant growth is desired twice weekly.

NOTE.—This remedy is non-poisonous and easily washed off. As its work is done through and not on the skin, care should be taken that the affected animal is kept out of cold air and draughts for some hours after the lotion has been applied. So marvellous are the hair-producing powers, that it is most urgent in cases where short hair is a desirability on face and ears (such as show Poms) to use the lotion sparingly, and stop all applications as soon as the desired quantity of hair has been obtained.

4/- per Bottle, post free.

BRUNNE, 11, GRESHAM ROAD, BRIXTON.

NOTICE.—Please Note that the Address on Page 168 should read as above.

TO AMERICANS.

MRS. JACKLIN,
OF BROOKLANDS,
WARWICK STREET,
AGGBRIGG, WAKEFIELD,

Will be very pleased to show her Pekingese to American or other visitors by appointment. They include some very beautiful young dogs, and puppies of the highest possible quality; also that lovely little

"SLEEVE DOG,"

Ashton-More Kwai-Yung

(By KWAI-KWAI OF EGHAM x ASHTON-MORE LINKA-TU).

His Pedigree is a combination of blood lines not often equalled.

:: :: STUD CARDS :: ::
and all further details on application.

————o·————

SHOW AND BREEDING STOCK
FOR SALE.

MRS. PRESTON-WHYTE'S SCHIPPERKES AND PEKINGESE,
At Langdale, Charlton Lane, Cheltenham.

By King Elf of Ashcroft x Borgie of Toddington.

Grand Sire— Prince Tuan of Toddington.

———

Only time shown took 6 Firsts, 6 Specials, and Special for best dog in the Show, only Pekingese being shown.

He has some handsome offspring, and throws, so far, quite small stock.

His weight is 9½ lbs., and he is a well-marked Grey brindle.

———

KING ELF of Ashcroft, also belongs to the Leigh Kennel, and there are several of his daughters and others of both sexes, all of good parentage.

LEIGH YUNG BOJUM.

MRS. PRESTON-WHYTE'S SCHIPPERKES AND PEKINGESE,

At Langdale, Charlton Lane, Cheltenham.

SCHIPPERKES I have had ever since 1894, and many other breeds of dogs, mostly sporting.   Pekingese are a newer fancy better suited to near a town, and I have had them now for 9 years or so.

MINNIE.　　　**LEIGH LIZETTE.**
By Ch. GRIZZLY BEAR.　　By LYN COUNT x LEIGH FANCY.
Grand Sire : Firwood Frolic.

LIZETTE is half-sister to Ch. Leigh Tommy Atkins, and is the las. of my winning strain of Schipperkes.   She has a raven black coat harsh with the real under coat, perfect legs and feet, short cobby body and well-rounded hind quarters, dark eyes and well-carried ears.

MINNIE is the same strain and equally black, but a little larger.

Mrs. PHILIP HUNLOKE'S PEKINGESE,

At Grenehurst Park, Capel, Surrey.   Phone: Capel 11.

Station : OCKLEY, half-mile, L.B. & S.C.R.

CH. WINGERWORTH CHIN-CHIN.

A beautiful little home-bred Particolour.

———

Winner of many Championships under all the leading Judges.

———

On her last appearance at the Kennel Clubs Show at the age of 10, she still carried all before her, and charmed the onlookers by her perfect ring manners and youthful appearance.

Mrs. HARRIS'S PEKINGESE, at 12, Spencer Gardens, Eltham, S.E.9.

MATILAL FOO-KWAI.

Sire—ASHTON-MORE FOO-KWAI. Red and white Particolour. Huge eyes. profuse coat and plume, and wonderful bone. Winner of 20 prizes at his first three shows, and Special for best coated Peke out of 20.

Fee - £5 5s.

DE-LA-POLE KENNELS, owned by Mr. and Mrs. ROBERT COX, 49, Albert Avenue, Newington, Hull.

DE-LA-POLE CHOPS
AT STUD.

Grand sire—Lyncroft Chops y. g. Broadoak Beetle. Dam—Galtee Peggy.

He is a dark Brindle, with broad skull, large eyes, very broad short face, square jaw, massive bone, good body and a profuse coat.

Born June 19th, 1919.

Siring lovely Puppies and is doing well in the Show Ring, having won every time shown, including Hull, Sheffield and Carlisle.

Fee for a short time, £3 3s.

Mrs. HAYES-SADLER'S PEKINGESE,
At 10, Colinette Road, Putney.   Tel. Putney 2079.

NORSBURY BINGO.

Clear cream, black eyes and nose.   Sire, Boltonia Chong;   Dam, Chilland Panzi.

CHILLAND PHILIP.

Fawn, black mask.   Weight 5lb.   Sire, Chilland Chu Lu; Dam, Chilland Polly.

BENNI OF WEI HEI.

Winner three Championships—Placed among ţthe six best dogs in the show, competing for the Lonsdale Cup at the Kennel Club Show November 3rd, 1920.   Weight 10½lbs.

CHILLAND PANZI.

Red brindle, black mask.   Sire, Benni of Wei Hei ; Dam, Wen Lu of Wei Hei.

Mrs. PATERSON-WALDIE'S PEKINGESE,

At Priorwood, Polton, Midlothian.   Phone 55 Lasswade.

PRIORWOOD PETAL
(at 15 months).

Bright red, by TSAN PAM OF CHINATOWN ex MIMOSA OF CHINATOWN.

Winner of the following prizes :—

Manchester—Five Firsts & One Second under Mrs. Raymond Mallock.

Pekingese Club Show—Second Open under 8ibs., under Mrs. Browning.

Blackpool—One First, Two Seconds, Reserve Championship, under Mrs. Slingsby.

Carlisle—Two Seconds, under Mrs. R. A. Gibbons.

Scottish Kennel Club—Three Firsts, and Championship, under Mrs. Holder.

Mrs. PATERSON-WALDIE'S PEKINGESE,
At Priorwood, Polton, Midlothian.   Phone 55 Lasswade.

PRIORWOOD PODGER.

Fawn dog by TSAN PAM OF CHINATOWN and PRIORWOOD POLLYOOLY
(Litter sister to Ch. Priorwood Pagan).

He is a clear golden fawn, huge eyes, very short bowed legs,
grand body and very short face.   Sire of most wonderful puppies.

———

FEE (at present) - 5 Guineas.

Mr. and Mrs. WILSON'S PEKINGESE,
At Bank Buildings, Rawson Street, Halifax.

Photo by]   [*Fall.*

ASHTON-MORE OUEN-LOO.

A beautiful red brindle dog, with massive head, immense bone, and a wonderful coat.   Bred in the purple.

His pedigree being a combination of the following noted dogs :

CH. NANKING WENTI.
CH. CHINKY CHOG.
CH. CHUERH OF ALDERBOURNE
CH. CHOO TAI OF EGHAM.
TOTO OF NOKE.
WEE WONG OF WESTBURY.

FEE - - - £5.

THE "UDNEY" PEKINGESE.

AT STUD.

**The Property of Miss I. A. LORD, "Sunnydene,"
25, Larkfield Road, Richmond, Surrey.**

Photo by]   *[Thos. Fall.*

ASHTON-MORE LI-WONG
(Photo taken at 9 months old.)

K.C.S.B. No. 20577.

Possesses immense coat, exceptionally low to ground
with splendid legs.

FEE - - - 3 Guineas.

SHIRRA POYANG.

Winner of **23** prizes, including **eight** firsts and **twice** best Peke in show at five shows. Siring lovely red puppies with black masks, fee 5gns., other studs from 3gns., also winning Japanese, photos and particulars.

C. FARNEY-BROWN, 4, Colbourne Road, Brighton.

Miss CROUCHER'S GRIFFONS

(Continued from Page 203).

Bettine of Rippington was only 10 months when photo was taken. She is by Tommie ex Cherisette of Sunny Mede. At Kensington and L.K.A. Mems she took 1st, two 2nds, three 3rds and a special. · Miss Croucher's other bitches are also prize winners, and are Bonfire of Rippington by Ch. Copthorne Firebrand and Thundersley Midget by Coquelicot ex Rosie, who in addition to being a prize winner herself was the mother of the 1st prize litter and her son ·(previous litter) was 1st (Puppies) at Richmond, July, 1920.

CORRECTIONS.

The sire of Mrs. Gibbons's Mongol Dah-Rub should be Mongol Yaou Jin. Her Yu-Whang of Frere is by Sunden T'sung-Tao ex a daughter of Ashton-More Chu-Chis and her Anita of Frere is by the late Chilland Chu-Lu ex Alresford Mimosa by Sutherland Ave. Kuei (see page 154). ————

FREEMAN'S CAPSULES—IMPORTANT NOTICE.

Since going to press we have received a notice from Messrs. Freeman's ·that they have altered the classification of their Worm Capsules, so the doses mentioned on page 112 are no longer correct. When ordering Capsules in future, the weight of dog should be given.

BOLTONIA LI H'SUN.

AT STUD.

Boltonia Li H'sun. Born April, 1917. Weight 8¼lbs.

Sire—Li of Chinatown. Dam—Momo of Chinatown.

Winner of numerous First prizes.

Special for best headed Pekingese, Llanwrst, 1919.

Sire of winning Puppy, Llanwrst, 1920, and many other very
promising youngsters.

He is a perfect lion-shaped dog with massive head, glorious eyes,
splendid bone, excellent tail carriage and profuse coat and feathering.

Fee 5 Guineas.

Bitches to Church, L. Y. R. Station.

—— ——

Mrs. F. GRAHAM MOORE, Stanhill Villa, Oswaldtwistle,
near Accrington.

THE WITTON PEKINGESE, property of Miss TURNER-HACKWOOD, "Riversleigh," Rectory Road, Beckenham, Kent.

KIN OF WITTON
Son of Brackley Kinchau.   Weight 5½lbs.   Proved sire

RASTUS OF WITTON
Son of Kin of Witton.   Weight 7½lbs.   Golden red, with big black mask; superb legs and very low to ground.   Proved sire of marvellous-headed puppies.

Miss Turner-Hackwood has five Stud Dogs, all tiny lovely Puppies. Different strains to suit all Bitches.

THE WITTON PEKINGESE, property of Miss TURNER-HACKWOOD, "Riversleigh," Rectory Road, Beckenham, Kent.

A Witton Matron—GLORY OF WITTON.
Dam of some exquisite puppies.

JEFF,
A rising Witton stud, age 6 months, sire Yuk Yuk of Witton.

The Witton Dogs are not entered in Shows on account of distemper.
PUPPIES USUALLY FOR SALE.

"**VERITY LE GRANDFILS**," 6lbs. weight, evenly broken red and white parti, grandson of the late Verity Buti Boi. At Stud, fee **7 Gns.**

AT STUD.

REMENHAM BENIE,

Fee, 7 Guineas.

ALSO

ZANZA,

Handsome biscuit son of **Faraline Ching Ah Ling.** Heavy bone, black mask. Siring lovely small puppies.

Fee, 5 Guineas.

Mrs. A. BORLEY,

The Cedars, Esher, Surrey. 'Phone: 178 Esher.

244

THE GREYSTONE PEKINGESE.

Photo by]   **PRINCE FU OF GREYSTONES.**   [*Stickyhaoles, Dublin*

Son of the late Ta-Fo of Greystones.   A fawn brindle, black mask.

Under 7lbs.   Photo taken at 18 months.

Fee - **12 guineas.**

BILLY OF GREYSTONES - - - - - Fee, **10 guineas.**

WAN YU OF TODDINGTON - - - - Fee, **7 guineas.**

KIN TA TING OF GREYSTONES - - - Fee, **7 guineas.**

Other young dogs, Stud Fees, 5 guineas.

ADULTS AND PUPPIES ALWAYS FOR SALE.

Apply—**Miss HEUSTON,**

St. David's, Greystones, Co. Wicklow.

Mrs. H. HUTLEY'S PEKINGESE,
At Well House, 57, Meadow Road, Leeds.

ASHTON-MORE SHOH-DEE

Born 17th June, 1919, is a son of Ashton-More Chu-Chi. Wolf sable, with a terrific head, broad muzzle, large eyes, flat face, lovely coat and feathering. A suitable dog for weak faced Bitches.

Fee for short time, **2 Guineas.**

FI-YEN

Is a son of Buscoe Beetle, grandson of Ch. Broadoak Beetle. Jet black, with white front, short cobby little dog, carries a profuse coat, has large dark eyes, short face, well bowed legs.

Fee for first six Bitches, **2 Guineas.**

Mrs. H. HUTLEY'S PEKINGESE,

At Well House, 57, Meadow Road, Leeds.

Mrs. H. HUTLEY has not advertised her kennels since 1914, but in the meantime has been building up again, and now places at stud three of her beautiful dogs.

PUPPIES USUALLY FOR SALE.

ASHTON-MORE HOO-MUM

Born 30th April, 1919, is a magnificent son of Ashton-More Phantom, grandson of Ch. Phantom of Ashcroft. Glorious red, black mask, large eyes, flat short face, grand front, short bowed legs. Weight 7lbs.

Fee - - **2 Guineas.**

LYNCROFT CHIN-CHIN.   Fee **5** Guineas.

SUZANNE OF CRAIGLEA.
By the late Verity Beauti Boi.

WAN-YEH OF CRAIGLEA (weight 4lbs.).
Fawn brindle by Lyncroft Chin-Chin by Ch. Broadoak Beetle.
Fee, 10 guineas.

DAFFODIL OF CRAIGLEA.
Bright red with black mask, by Thres of Craiglea ex Too Dee of
Craiglea.

249

DON JUAN OF ASHCROFT

Winner of 1st and special, beating championship winners. Lovely small dog, 8lb. Rich red, grand head, absolutely flat face, no nose, extra short body and legs. Fee, **5** guineas.

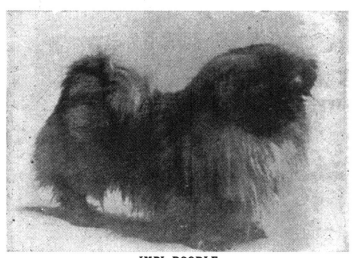

IMPI DOODLE

Golden sable. The lovely grandson of Ch. Broadoak Beetle. Magnificent head, short legs and body, 9lbs. Fee, **3** guineas. At stud in London by arrangement.

PEKOE OF EASTDOWN.

1st, 2nd, 3rd and Special Prizewinner, under Mrs. KINGHAM (his first show), February, 1920.

A lovely red, with black mask.   Sire of exceptionally good puppies.

Sire, "Wong Sing of Westbury," by "Wee Wong of Westbury," and a daughter of "Sutherland Avenue H'Sin."

Dam, by "Portlet Kinchau," son of "Brackley Kinchau."

LU JOSS TIEN OF MEADHURST.
Handsome red brindle, siring very small puppies.
By Champion Tien Joss of Greystones.   **Fee 5 Guineas.**

MITTOU OF MEADHURST.   By Champion Chu-êrh Tu of
Alderbourne.   A lovely miniature (war baby).   **Fee 5 Guineas.**

Mr. H. M. BRIGGS (GLENORME) PEKINGESE.
At Bodalaw, Church Walks, Llandudno.

E WO RIKKY DIKKY. Stud Book No. 159 Z.
Born, Nov. 1916.   Breeder, Mrs. Jardine Gresson.
Sire E Wo Tu ex E. Wo Ki-Ki.
He is a proved sire of beautiful puppies.   Fee **5** Guineas.

To American Visitors.

Miss ANSON, at 15, De Beauvoir Square, Dalston, London, N., extends a cordial invitation to all American Visitors to visit her kennels.   She will be most pleased to show them her beautiful dogs by appointment.   Miss Anson is well known as the breeder of the beautiful Prince Cha, sold by Miss Ashton Cross for a big sum to America. Miss Anson still owns his sire Lu Chun, and has others of the same strain in her kennels, and can always supply show and breeding stock of the highest quality.

DOGS AT STUD from 2 Guineas.

253

THE
ECCLESALL STUD PEKINGESE

THE PROPERTY OF

Mrs. CLARK and Miss NEWMAN,

At 249, Ecclesall Road, Sheffield.

———

T'SAN WANG OF ECCLESALL

A lovely red dog with a massive skull, broad flat face, level mouth. He carries a tremendous coat and fringes and lovely plume, very heavy bone, well bowed front and exceptionally low to ground—a true Peke in every way. As a sire he is proving a great success, his first litter winning first prize in strong competition at the Northern Counties Peke Club.

———

Fee   -   -   -   -   £3 3s.

for a short time only.

PRIORWOOD PERKI.
A lovely-headed fawn bitch.
Winner at the Edinburgh Championship Show, and at Leith, best
bitch in Show.

Mrs. PATERSON WALDIE'S PEKINGESE,

At Priorwood, Polton, Midlothian.

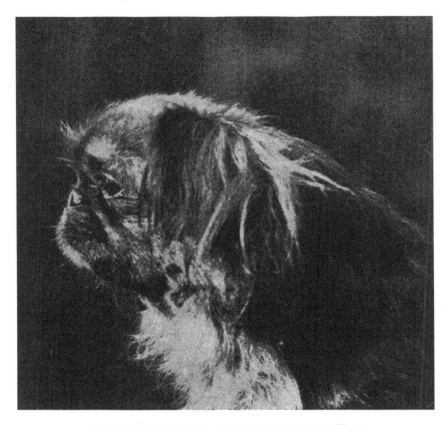

PRIORWOOD PI (late Ashton-More Chinky Chog).

By Dimbie of Burton on Dee ex Eva.   Red Brindle.

Always admitted by experts to be the best-headed Peke in Scotland.

He has wonderful bone, short well-bowed legs and a perfect figure.

Fee   -   -   £4 4s.

Mrs. PATERSON WALDIE'S PEKINGESE,

At Priorwood, Polton, Midlothian.

PRIORWOOD PHLUNRUSH.

By Priorwood Panther ex Hyena Owlett.   Black and Tan.

Wonderful head, perfectly flat face, huge eyes, heavy bone, grand front, a real lion shaped body and an immense coat. A well-known winner and excellent sire.

Fee   -   -   -   -   £5 5s.

258

A Dainty Diet
for
A Dainty Dog.

TOY DOGS require right housing, right grooming and washing, and above all, right feeding if they are to be maintained in the good health which makes them pleasurable companions. No diet so suits the constitutions of small dogs of this kind than

SPRATT'S
—OVALS—

varied frequently by feeds of

SPRATT'S
PET-RODNIM.

Sold by dealers throughout the world.

"DOG CULTURE" contains 64 pages of valuable information about dogs in general and Toy Dogs in particular. Write now for a free copy to——— Spratt's Patent Limited, 24/5, Fenchurch St., London, E.C.3.

Printed by The Southern Publishing Co., Ltd., Brighton, England.

Lightning Source UK Ltd.
Milton Keynes UK
UKHW011523190620
365269UK00002B/513